1

This Book is Dedicated to My Late Father,

# Richard (Dick) Clemens

Every time I think of you and start to get sad, I remember something silly you said or did and I end up laughing.

I hope my writings are giving you some laughs, Dad, Wherever you are.

Book Cover by

# Tamberlee King

You never cease to amaze me and I can't thank you enough!

And a special thank you to

# Brian King

For coming up with yet another brilliant subtitle.

# Fifty

# Shades

# Of

# African

# Grey

## Georgi Abbott

## *Introduction*

This is the fourth published book I have written about Pickles and is similar to the first two books – Pickles The Parrot and Pickles The Parrot Returns. I have kept it to mostly humorous stories about Pickles and his life with us. Pickles tells some of the stories himself because sometimes it's just better coming from him when he talks about what it's like to be a parrot, the frustrations of dealing with humans, his deep and twisted mind and confused thoughts about living with his pain-in-the-ass Mom, his wonderful Dad, his little dog and life in general.

# The Indignity of it All!

My work area is a combination computer room/guest room and I'm in it most of the day and sometimes I'll work late into the evening and just fall into bed there, rather than wake Neil when I go to bed in our room. Neil has an area in the diningroom that he uses for his office and it's also where we have a bunch of ropes and boings set up for Pickles so Pickles spends a lot of time in there with Daddy when he's working at home, which he does a fair amount of the time. Now and then, throughout the day, Neil will bring Pickles in to visit me and Neil will lay on the bed while Pickles looks around, talks to me, gets scratches from Neil or maybe he'll take a little nap beside Dad.

On this particular day, Neil was lying down with his head on the pillow while Pickles perched on the edge of the bed; butt in the air, watching Neeka Dog on the floor – Pickles that is, not Neil. I had stopped working and leaned back in my chair to visit with them when suddenly Pickles flapped straight up in the air, about 3 feet, and came back down facing Neil and right in front of his face. I burst out laughing because it looked so silly and Neil's eyes were going cross-eyed staring back at Pickles, about 6 inches away. "What the heck was THAT all about?" I asked Pickles through my laughter. Neil answered for him and I lost it and fell off my chair laughing when he explained that while Pickles' butt was all up in his face, he noticed a loose little downy feather hanging near his twinker so he tried to blow it off. All Pickles knew was that somebody was blowing up his butt and this just wouldn't do! Actually, I don't think Pickles quite knew what had happened except that something had come from Dad's general direction but because he had no proof about anything, he left Dad's lips intact.

*I was sitting on the kitchen counter watching Mom and Dad prepare supper and Mom was holding a carrot in her hands while talking to Dad. I got a little angry because I always get a piece of carrot while they are chopping it up but now I was getting impatient with them ignoring my nutritional needs so at first I was going to steal a big bite but then I jumped up on the carrot at the last second and found that it made a really good snackery perch so I started eating it while I was perching on it. I'm going to get Dad to make a whole bunch of carrot perches for me – but not bell pepper perches because I tried one of those next and as much as you want to chew through them to get to the yummy seed core, you can't help but slide right off those suckers.*

## Noisy Bird

It's funny what each person considers bothersome noise. Barking dogs, gas motors on a lake and children bother me most. I don't like other people's dogs barking and it particularly bothers me when my own bark because I'm so conscious of the barking bothering other people. There's nothing worse than being out in nature, listening to the birds or merely enjoying the peace and quiet while others are driving gas powered boats, ATV's or dirt bikes. Noise from children can be like nails on a chalkboard for me, and it doesn't matter if they are happy noises or crying and screaming noises – they bother me equally. I don't like being like that but I just can't help it.

People are always asking me if parrots are noisy and the only answer I can give is, 'no, not for me'. I just don't hear it anymore because to me, it's not an unpleasant noise. I mean, I DO hear it and love listening to Pickles but it's easily tuned out as background noise when I'm preoccupied. We get a fair amount of visitors and often people stay for a few days because we live in a remote town in the middle of the province and I don't ever remember anybody complaining about the noise Pickles makes. Mind you, I suppose houseguests aren't likely to complain when they are visiting but they tend to keep coming back. However, when we had the flyshop all those years and used to take Pickles to work with us, now and then people would remark that having a parrot around would bother them because they seemed noisy. Understandable.

I had a woman stop me on the trail one day while I was walking Neeka Dog on the leash with Pickles in his backpack on my back, and she asked me, "Aren't parrots awfully noisy?" "Not at all" I answered, "Well, not Pickles anyway. I mean, sure he makes noise but not near as much as kids playing, yelling, crying, squealing etc. Pickles mostly likes to talk in a normal voice, sing songs, whistle beautifully, copy wild birds (only louder), copy electronic sounds, stuff like that. He never screams for attention and only now and then does this annoying little squawk when he's not happy. So, as far as I'm concerned – no, he's not noisy at all."

The whole time I was talking, Neeka and Pickles were barking at a family of Marmots who were sunbathing on a large rock a few feet away. Neeka was barking his little dog yap and Pickles was using the neighbor's Great Dane bark. I ordered everybody to be quiet and eventually Neeka stopped, reluctantly, but Pickles continued because he doesn't obey the 'be quiet' command since we never use it with him. And then, since Pickles wouldn't stop, I guess Neeka decided it was hardly fair that he should stop when Pickles didn't have to so he started barking again.

In the end, not only did I look like a bad pet owner who couldn't control her animals, but also Pickles made me look like a liar about him not being noisy. Then, to top it off, as we parted Pickles did the ambulance siren down the trail and around the bend.

*Mom asked me if I wanted some banana for lunch. I love banana but when I opened my mouth to tell her, "yes, please" – "Go poop potatoes" came out instead. Mom told me I had just talked my way out of a banana lunch and that I should think before speaking. I understand that I blew it and now had to suffer the lunch consequences but on the other hand, I don't like to think before I speak because I like to be just as surprised as everyone else by what comes out my mouth.*

## Doing, Doing, Doing, Doing

Good friends of mine, Warren and Doris, came to visit for a couple of days and they were constantly jumping up and running to their cell phone. Each time, there was nobody there and no message left to show that someone had called. I wasn't really paying attention and they only mentioned it in passing so nobody really thought anything of it until, while Doris was holding her phone, Pickles went "Doing, doing, doing, doing". "He's doing my ring tone!" Doris hollered. "Oh my God!" I said, "THAT'S where he got that sound!"

He'd been doing that sound for about four months – the exact amount of time since Doris last visited – and it reminds me of a cartoon pogo stick sound. It had been driving us nuts, trying to figure out where Pickles had picked the sound up. Well, now we finally knew however, it didn't stop Doris and

Warren from running to their phone each time they heard it.

(Look for the video of Pickles doing this sound on You Tube as 'Pickles The Parrot – Doing, Doing')

*For crying out loud, Pickles, perhaps next time you fly, you will remember that that ornament cannot hold your weight and that by landing on it, it will crash to the ground, scaring you all to hell. Mom, one thing you should know about me by now is that I don't learn lessons.*

### Crazy Lady

I decided to take Pickles on a little outing so I packed him up in his backpack and we drove up town to take a short walk around the lake with Neeka Dog. We had a nice little walk and then we sat on a bench overlooking the water and there was not a single soul around for Pickles to embarrass me in front of. He was quite content to caw at the ducks and show off his other wild bird repertoire.

After walking back to the car, we drove across the street to the outdoor mall so I could pick up the mail at the post office. I put Pickles on my back again for the short walk and on the way back, he started with the wolf whistles and his doing, doing, doing sounds just as we were approaching some people who were sitting on a bench in the common area.

Instead of stopping to explain, as I usually do when people can't see Pickles because I'm facing them with him hidden in back, I decided to keep walking, as I knew that in a moment I would be past them and the backpack would be self-explanatory. When I arrived at the car a minute later, I removed the backpack to place it in the car and that's when I noticed that Pickles had pulled up all the paper from the bottom of the cage and then climbed down to the bottom, effectively hiding himself beneath and behind the paper.

That means nothing was explained to those people and instead, I just looked like some weirdo walking through the mall, whistling and doinging with a backpack full of old newspaper. Soon, if Pickles has his way, the town will declare me crazy and unfit to own a bird.

*Mom and Dad never yell at me to shut up – mostly because I hardly ever annoy them with obnoxious sounds, but also because they know that yelling at a parrot doesn't work and usually only makes it worse. But today I was being so abnormally loud, obnoxious and miserable that they were at their wits ends and lost all patience and poise and yelled at me, in stereo, to "Shut the heck up!" At first I was totally shocked and Mom said my jaw even dropped in surprise but then I realized how cool it was and broke into happy song for the next ½ hour, hoping they would do it again but they didn't. Then I realized that they would probably only repeat that behavior if I made really annoying sounds again so that's what I did for the rest of the day until supper time but I never did get a replay out of them. Being obnoxious is totally boring if nobody's paying attention.*

### Laughing at Pickles' Expense – Scary

What is it with African Greys and their fears and phobias? Pickles will freak out over the dumbest things and then, the things he *should* be afraid of, he takes completely in stride. We tried to introduce him to everything possible when he was young, and as he was growing up, but you can't do it with everything in the world. Besides, something that was totally familiar to him a year ago can suddenly turn monster during its short absence.

There is 'frightening' and then there is 'startling' and while both can be very bothersome for both bird and bird owner, 'startling' is usually the most entertaining – for me, mostly. Like the time that Pickles had climbed down from his cage and was busy inspecting a bug on the floor. As I walked over to get him he started to reach for the bug with an open beak and with his tongue reaching and wiggling hesitantly in his mouth in anticipation of what it might taste or feel like and before I could contain myself, I freaked and yelled at him. Poor Pickles. I startled him in to running, and he was pretty sure by now that the bug had something to do with it and, while trying to avoid it, he tripped over the bug in his haste to flee. Then, to top it off, he screamed like a little girl when he realized he had made skin contact.

Another time, I was working on my computer in my office and I could hear the little clicking sounds his talons make when he's walking on the floor. I decided to ignore him long enough to finish a thought in a story I was writing and to allow him to think that his stealth was keeping him from being discovered. The clicking sounds started to get closer so I knew he was heading down the hall towards me so I watched, out of the corner of my eye, as he appeared in the doorway, stopped, and then proceeded to cross out of my sight and continue down the hall with his slow motion chicken walk and exaggerated head and neck movements with each step, looking over at me with the same 'pretend I'm not watching you' look that I was giving him, out of the corner of *his* eye. Neeka Dog had been following Pickles – I could tell by the slightly heavier clicks his own nails produced on the floor – and while

13

Pickles was surely thinking he had a partner in crime, Neeka had decided to turn on him and rat him out. Pickles wasn't expecting this mutiny, or the sudden loud noise mid-stride and half way to freedom so one quick, sharp yap shot him straight up in the air and straight into my room. Covert operation foiled.

I got a bonus that day when I picked him up from there and took him to hang out on the couch in front of the window. Pickles was sitting on the back of the couch, laughing at a Waxwing perched on a fence post a few feet away. Suddenly, the Waxwing up and flew straight into the window! In the split second, just before it hit, Pickles had a look on his face as if thinking, "What a stupid bird!" but then when it hit the window with a bang, it scared the crap out of him and he jumped up in a big flap and smacked right into the window himself!

I should say here that Pickles is very good about windows; he's aware of them. There are a couple of windows in the house that he's not used to and when he's been startled, he will head toward them but pull up at the last moment and actually try to land on them but of course he kinda slides down in a crumpled heap. At least, I think he's window savvy but it's probably just a testament to my housekeeping practices and window cleaning skills, or lack of. But in this last incidence, I have no idea what that was all about. I think he just has no sense of direction when startled – just like the time I sneezed him right into the dog dish. He was napping on his ropes in the diningroom when I suddenly sneezed my nose and the next thing Pickles knew, he was dog food.

Mind you, a good sense of direction did him no good at all another time when Neil was sleeping on the couch and Pickles got bored but decided not to disturb Daddy (he's very good about these things) and opted to go looking for me instead. I heard his clicking nails go through the kitchen and just as he was heading down the hall, I got up to go fetch him. Pickles hadn't expected me to appear through the doorway and he screamed in surprise, flapped up into the air and around my head, which startled me because it all happened so fast and I wasn't expecting the ruckus so I screamed too, which startled Pickles into another scream as he turned tail and flew into the livingroom where he landed in Dad's hair which shocked Dad into jumping up with a shout and sending Pickles falling to the floor which sent Pickles screaming and running across the floor and back up his cage where he turned to stare at us as if thinking, 'My God, you'd think they'd never seen a bird before!"

I know I'm terrible but I can't help but laugh at some of Pickles' misfortunes. Sometimes he's like a little kid that gets hurt or scared but when they see people laughing, their desire to entertain takes over and they will laugh right along with you. Sometimes it doesn't work though and my laughing sometimes seems to make him feel abashed, and sometimes the embarrassment will cause him to get angry. Doesn't matter though, I still find it funny – and what I find funniest of all, is when he informs me himself that something is, "Scary!" He doesn't usually say it though until he has settled down from the scare, safe and puffy cheeked.

He definitely informed me it was 'Scary' the day he was sitting on his boing in the diningroom while I did dishes in the kitchen. He was being silly and talking some strange, loud garbled language when a spider dropped suddenly from the ceiling and stopped right in front of his face, dangling on its web strand. He immediately flipped out, flapped his wings frantically to make a wind to carry it away while emitting the blood curdling Grey scream to scare the crap out of it. I don't know where the spider ended up and I'm as scared of spiders as Pickles is so I wasn't about to look for it among his ropes and toys; he was on his own. But the spider was out of sight and that was all that mattered to Pickles as he fluffed up, told me how 'scary' it was and sat contemplating the whole bad experience and probably wondering if the garbled language had somehow summoned the spider to begin with.

He yelled, "Scary!" at me several times from atop his cage one night when I approached him with his freshly washed sheet for covering his cage. I had it folded up in my hands and was about to shake it out to cover him up because he had informed me he wanted to go to bed but before I could do that, he ran to the back of the top of the cage and yelled, "Scary! Stop it!" When I finally got it unfolded into one large body, he immediately settled down and told me to turn his 'lights off'. Sheet folded into a small bundle – scary. Sheet unfurled to about fifty times the size of the bundle – totally cool, man.

I felt bad one time though. I put a few pine nuts in a small, clear container for him to play as a maraca or remove the snap lid to eat the treats but he decided he was scared of it. I'd given him this sort of thing hundreds of times over the years but not recently so he decided it was a little scary. I placed it in his sleeping tent, figuring he'd slowly approach it sometime during the day but then I forgot about it. That night I covered him up for bedtime and it wasn't until the next morning that I realized it was still in the tent and that Pickles had been too scared to sleep in there all night. I hope he wasn't sitting on a perch in the corner, sleeping with one eye open for fear the container would grow legs and come for him in the middle of the night.

To be afraid of something new is one thing but to be afraid of something just because it has been moved from one position to another, is another thing entirely. I removed the playstand next to Pickles' cage in the livingroom because I wanted to find something smaller so that his cage and play area weren't taking up half the livingroom. I struggled to pull it out of the livingroom and then left it sitting in the middle of the diningroom until Neil came home to pull it all apart. A little later, I went to fetch Pickles to bring him to his diningroom ropes but the moment he spotted the playstand, he started flapping and leaning back on my hand, afraid to go any closer. It took me all afternoon to reacquaint him with the playstand that he's had for ten years and just when I finally got him to sit on it so he could look out the window, I hit the corner of it with my hip as I was walking away and off Pickles flew, never to return to the stand again.

A few days later, I took down all his diningroom ropes so I could wash them and, like I always do when I put them back, I change them around to make it more interesting to Pickles. Again, when I approached the ropes with him on my hand, he started leaning back on my hand, afraid to go any closer. Pickles can't stand it if someone is cleaning or fixing things on his cage or play areas so I held him way out to one side and then lied to him about how the bells and toys had to be fixed and got busy with my other hand, pretending to adjust things. Pickles stopped leaning away and stood staring at my hand activity. Soon he started leaning *toward* the ropes so I, ever so slowly, moved that hand toward the ropes. Now he couldn't get there quick enough and he started splaying his wings, impatient because I wasn't moving him fast enough. Finally, he was close enough to hop on to a rope and

17

scamper up to my hand to help fix a bell by nibbling my fingers, hanging upside down on them and trying to feed my thumb.

You would think he would be most afraid of thunder storms but because we made a party of them when he was little by getting all excited and going 'woo hoo!' every time there was thunder, Pickles thinks it's great fun. To him, it's good music with lots of bass and has a beat you can dance to.

*Jeez, Pickles – the things you do and say in front of people make me blanch. I felt sorry for you because you've been cooped up in the house all winter and I was just trying to be nice by taking you shopping with me in your birdie backpack. Two minutes into the store and you start insulting people by calling them 'poop butts' and embarrassing me with fart sounds, making people think it's me that's farting because they can't see you on my back when I'm facing them. If you don't start behaving nicely while we're out, I'm going to stop taking you anywhere. Do you understand what I'm saying, Pickles? Yes, Mom – everything except the part where you changed your name to Blanche. That's it; you're on a time out - see you later, Pickles. Okay, see ya Blanche.*

### Wanna Go For a Walk?

Pickles is getting lazy. When he wants to go for a walk, he just lifts his foot to step up. I decided he had to start asking again so I kept asking if he wanted to go for a walk and when he didn't repeat it, I'd say, "No?" and just walk away. I'd sit on the couch and ask him from there but he still wouldn't repeat it. Then I realized the mistake I'd made. I had to go out soon and if Pickles didn't ask to go for a walk pretty quick, I would have to either reward his stubbornness by having him step up for a walk while I still had time, or I'd have to deprive him of his walk after getting him so excited about it. Or, what if he finally said it just as I was walking out the door and now he has to be rewarded, making me late for my appointment?

I opted for distracting him with some over exaggerated phoniness. "LOOK, Pickles! What's that outside?? Oh my God, Oh my God!! Wanna see? LET'S GO SEE!! Step up – GOOD BOYYYY!" and off we went to look at nothing out the window. But as far as he knew, we were just too late, we had missed it and he's kicking himself because he didn't step up just a little bit faster. And he hasn't time to think, "Heyyy, I didn't ask to go for a walk and yet I still got to go for a walk. Guess I don't have to say it after all – and just as I was almost gonna say it anyway. Phew!"

So then we go for our walkabout. We ended up in the back room, checking out the tomato and pepper plants that Neil gets growing under UV lamps early in spring for fear of losing them to frost, which is possible right into July. As I'm checking the plants for dead leaves to pluck, Neeka trots through the room and slap slap, through the doggy door and outside. Pickles almost fell off my hand in surprise; why, Neeka just disappeared into thin air!

It struck me that all these years, Pickles had never happened to be back in this little room when a dog (or, a few years ago, cats) came through the flap in the door.

I had to laugh and I had to milk this a bit so I called Neeka right back in and Pickles nearly hit the roof at Neeka's amazing appearance from out of

19

nowhere! I ordered Neeka back outside as I took Pickles to the window so he could see Neeka on the porch. This was just too much for Pickles! He was pacing on my hand and leaning first one way, then the other because he couldn't figure out which way to guide me so that he could solve this amazing puzzle. I don't know what went on in his head, or if he understood that the back porch was accessible through the door in the back room but regardless, we can never go in that room anymore without Pickles getting all jumpy, expecting something to appear out of nowhere again.

It just wouldn't be a walk around the house without stopping to hang out on the bed. He wasn't interested in building forts out of the blankets on this trip; he was more interested in snagging my reading glasses off the night table. I didn't think he could reach them but here I was trying to pry them out of his beak before he could snap them in half. After I took them from him I went to his toy bureau, got him a pair of his own glasses (I buy children's sunglasses in packages of ten) and handed them to him to play with. They weren't forbidden fruit so he didn't want them. Instead, he spent the remainder of our bed time, staring down the gap between the bed and the wall.

You would think that would be a scary thing to him; looking into the deep, dark unknown. Even *I'M* afraid of things that might lurk under a bed. Never in my lifetime have I ever been able to dangle a foot over the edge of the bed for fear of what might grab it from below. But there's Pickles, the same Pickles who's afraid of his own feathers, just daring the monsters to come up from the abyss.

Now it's time to take him back so I can go out. I set him down on the top of his cage, hand him a walnut and as I walk out of the room I hear him softly say, "Wanna go for a walk?"

*Since I don't shower and merely sit on the shower rod, when you say, "Wanna go take a shower, Pickles?" I hear, "Wanna go chew up the walls, rod ends and shower curtain, Pickles?" and I'm like, duh, yeah.*

### The Toaster

After helping me make his supper each night, Pickles likes to ride the supper bowl back to his cage. Helping me make his supper means he gets to play on the counter and dance while I count the seconds that it's in the microwave (he thinks counting is a song) but he doesn't *always* get to go to the counter because sometimes we don't have the time to let him hang out or the counter isn't cleaned off. On this day, I wasn't planning to bring him out but when I went to get his dirty food and water bowls, he saw me coming and scrambled into his cage to sit on the bowl, basically giving me no choice but to pick him up with the bowl – not without a fight anyway. The little bugger knew where the bowl was going and was smart enough to hitch a ride.

Pickles has his own corner of the kitchen counter where we keep some talon toys and basically allow him to do what he wants there. The microwave is in a little pantry at that end, along with the hemp seed that goes in his supper bowl so that's where all the action is. Now and then we will allow him on the other counter but it means moving things like sugar bowls, butter, pens and paper, among other things, but he loves the toaster (unplugged) and on this day, I figured I'd give him a treat and change of scenery. A change of scenery for a few minutes is always great for putting him in a good mood for hours afterwards.

Immediately, he starts to chat it up with the toaster. It took me awhile to figure out why he runs around the counter saying 'Peek-a-boo', always with one eye on the toaster. Sometimes he just stands in front of it hollering 'Peek-a-boo', making me think he's a bit of a head case, until I realized what was going on.

Behind the toaster is the window between the kitchen and livingroom and the window is right next to Pickles' cage so that he can watch us from the perch we attached on the outside of the cage and nearest to the window. Naturally, he's almost always there when I'm making toast, which is almost every day and one morning, after the toast had popped up, I watched as Pickles got all excited and yelled, "Peek-a-boo!" a moment after the toast popped. So now, whenever he's on the toaster part of the counter, he figures if he hollers it long enough, toast will eventually pop up. I thought; this makes him both brilliant and dumb as nails.

You can watch Pickles riding his supper bowl on YouTube. It's called 'Pickles the Parrot Riding on Supper Bowl'.

*Mom was putting Christmas decorations in a box and I decided to fly over and help her but I missed the box completely and landed on her boob, upside down with my twinker in her face. "What the heck was that all about, Pickles?" she asked. "Scary!" I answered, cuz I think I got caught in her gravitational pull.*

# The Problems With Penises

If you've ready my books, you know of Neeka Dog's penis fetish but just to recap, Neeka is a rust colored, four year old, six pound Min Pin who came to live with us at 8 weeks old, when he could fit in the palm of a hand. He was endowed with a penis that was in no way proportionate to his body, being so large than a one-fingered belly rub was pretty much impossible without touching the offending appendage. His penis size grew less over time, his obsession with it didn't.

As a pup, he spent considerable time looking at it, cleaning it, appearing to listen to it and just generally checking to see if it was still there. As he grew older, it seemed he was conferring with it as if it had a mind of it's own and he was definitely blaming it for any trouble he found himself in. To this day, whenever he's being reprimanded, Neeka immediately turns and pokes the dick as if it were to blame for talking Neeka into it in the first place. He has never failed to do this. Not once.

He was neutered at six months of age (even though I prefer to wait longer because of possible physical developmental problems that could occur) and it was hoped that this would relieve some of the stress that his poor stuffies endured. The neutering made absolutely no difference – dry humping continued with zeal. At first, we didn't have the nerve to take them away from him for fear he'd use pillows or bunched up blankets or worse, our legs as substitution but eventually we did. It didn't matter though; he's so small that even the smallest toy will do.

I started wondering if the neutering didn't 'take', and if it was possible to have a second set of testicles hiding somewhere. I brought it up to the veterinarian during one of our visits for shots and found out that yes, some dogs are like that. Not only that, but they are actually capable of doing the deed with another dog. Great. Just freakin' great.

Because of all the dry humping he does with his stuffies, he tends to dry his penis out so that it won't retract back into the shaft and it ends up just flopping around, waving in the air and when it does this, it rubs against Neeka's chest, (Min Pins have those large under chests) perpetuates his excitement and, well, it's a vicious circle.

There was one episode that carried on for two days. Most of it had retracted but there was still some pink poking out. I was getting concerned so I was constantly poking at it, trying to push in or pull at the shaft to stretch it over the penis but it wasn't working. I thought; this can't be good. Then I decided it needed some lubrication and went to the store to buy some Vaseline. While I was there, I figured I'd better buy some bananas for Pickles so I grabbed both items and took them through the check out.

It wasn't until I was walking out of the story that I realized, in hindsight, why people in line had had strange looks on their faces. I may never return to that store again but at least Pickes got his bananas for lunch and Neeka the Dog's dick was back where it belonged.

*I can tell if people are scared of parrots just by latching on to their fingers and grinding my beak for a couple of minutes.*

## Miserable Old Bird

Pickles was in an ornery mood. We both were because my mood is always a reflection of his. So, today we had a pissing match. He nagged me mercilessly and I snapped what I thought were clever, insulting comebacks. "Wanna go for a walk, Buggerbutt!" he demanded. "YOU'RE the Buggerbutt!" I retorted, suddenly feeling like I was five years old again.

"Wanna go for a walk!" he nagged. "You don't walk, you ride!" I snapped back. That was better. "Besides, you walk like a duck!" There, take that.

I guess I got the better of him cuz all he could come up with was a raspberry. HA! I thought, proudly, I'm smarter than a bird! It's really quite the accomplishment.

Then Pickles started squawking that brain stabbing, frustrating noise that makes you want to reciprocate by screaming some horrible sound back at him – to both drown him out and to give him a taste of his own medicine. But even if I had the heart to do that, I'd worry what the neighbors would think.

He kept bagging on me to take him outside to the aviary and I kept telling him I was too busy to go outside and baby-sit him. Nothing would appease him. Not toys, not food, not even pine nuts. Anything I handed him, he threw in my face with a curse. I got called poophead, butthead, potatohead, ratboy and a number of his very own made up swear words such as sprrgat, bukaput and something phlegmy sounding. It was so hard not to throw the food back in his face as I picked it off the floor. I always manage to keep

25

from acting on my evil thoughts (My evil thoughts are just that, only thoughts.) But it's getting harder and harder to ignore the evil little man on my shoulder. I go cross-eyed trying to look at him but I imagine him looking like a cross between a lizard and a parrot. "Go ahead" he says, "Do it. You know you want to. Look how he treats you. A little piece of corn won't hurt." But instead, I drop everything I'm doing and pack him in his little cage to take him to the aviary.

He's happy as stink now and just as I set him on an aviary branch, emergency vehicles sped though the town, sirens wailing. Pickles joined the chorus and Neeka added the mournful howl. The sirens are now long gone but Pickles has become the emergency vehicle and he carries on just as loud.

Sirens and howling dogs pierced the air of the neighborhood as all the neighbor dogs are easily incited, until Pickles got bored and demanded to go home. "You just freakin' got here Pickles! I dropped everything to please you and now you wanna go home??" but I packed him up and back we went.

I set the cage on the table while I went back outside to collect my coffee and book and when I returned, Pickles was sitting nicely, chatting to himself. I opened the cage door and asked him to step up but he wouldn't so I left him there for a few minutes and went off to get some stuff done. As I walked through the room on a mission, Pickles purred "Hello, BabyYo." "Oh, I forgot about you Pickles. Wanna step up now?" But when I went to get him, he refused again so I closed the cage door and took off again.

I offered to take him out a few more times over the next couple of hours but Pickles was happy in his tiny little cage and spent his time chirping, singing, napping or chatting to himself. I found myself singing and chatting to myself too as I carried on with my work and marveled at how his moods affect me so much.

Pickles reminded me to feed him at suppertime, "Supper in a beak?" he asked, so I made his supper and tried to take him home to his cage to eat. He wouldn't step up; he wanted supper right where he was. This is his travel cage and it's rigged with bowl set-ups so I placed his food and water inside with him and left him there for another half hour or so until he started demanding, "Lights off!" "You've gotta be kidding!" I said, but I threw a towel over him and left him for the night.

A beautiful outside aviary with toys, trees, birdbath and fountain, a nice big cage indoors full of toys, playstands and ropes throughout the house, all the freedom a little birdie could ask for but today it takes confinement in a cage he can barely turn around in to make him happy.

*Last night, when it was time to go to bed, I got all mixed up and just climbed inside my cage and waited for Mom to give me my bedtime almond snack. Mom said, "Are you going to bed? Aren't you gonna ask me to turn your lights off?" Oh my God! I scampered back out of my cage, ran to the top, reached my neck way up toward my UV light, said "Lights off" and made the sound of the little snap the light switch does and then climbed back inside my cage for my almond. Phew! What was I thinking? I almost upset the entire universe!*

## Fun With Food

Parrots can be so hard to please, food-wise. Pickles gets better, and less finicky, as he grows older but we still suffer 'incidents'. It's so strange how he likes something one day but despises it the next – or visa versa. I'm sure a lot of it depends on the grower, the time of season and perfect ripeness but sometimes it just doesn't make sense. For 10 years I've given him pieces of apple to throw at the wall or the dog and several times a month, he's never surprised me by eating it. I've tried applesauce, at the expense of my clothing and furniture and apple juice that he completely changes his mind about every few months.

One day, while indulging in some applesauce myself, I offered Pickles some off my spoon. He grabbed the spoon in his beak before I had a chance to get a good grip and sent it flying into the TV but at the split second it was flying out of his mouth, I could see by the look on his face that he was wishing he hadn't done that because FINALLY it appeared as if science had come up with a palatable apple dish. He wanted it back and explained this with a whiny, "oooohhhhhhhhh" with his head cocked, staring at the spoon. When I offered it to him again, he took great scoops of it, swallowing as fast as he could, head bobbing and eyes pinning in ecstasy.

He continued to accept apples sauce offerings so I decided to push my luck and give him a small apple wedge. Pickles snapped it from my hand with his beak, held it with one talon and took a small, hesitant bite then made as if to toss it but it was like his talons wouldn't obey and let go. He held it out as far as his leg would take it and leaned his head and neck as far as possible in the opposite direction. His foot started to spasm and jerk up and down and back and forth in revulsion until he finally gave up, brought the apple to his mouth, eyes pinning as he devoured the whole wedge. This is the first time, in over 10 years, that Pickles has eaten apple without me hiding it in his birdie bread. The first time he as ever eaten a *fresh* one and I am happy to report that weeks and weeks have gone by and he is still thrilled to receive a wedge of apple, any kind of apple, as often as is offered. This is wonderful because apples contain much less sugar that other fruits.

I found out there's another food that will end in spoon tossing, and that's rice pudding. Pickles likes rice and he often asks for pudding – which is usually jars of baby food consisting of a mixture of pure pureed fruits with no additives or any other ingredient – but one day Neil made rice pudding and offered Pickles a taste. Pickles looked at the spoon, looked up at Daddy all confused but had no reason not to trust him so he took a small bite. He rolled it around with his tongue, testing taste and texture, as the true nature of this food slowly dawned on his face. Rice does not belong in pudding, rice is not a dessert but most of all, dessert should never contain 'supper'! What treachery is this? Off goes the spoon and all it's contents, landing on tonight's TV schedule.

Pickles has never been a big fan of broccoli but, unlike the first ten years of apple, he has nibbled the flower part on occasion. But mostly it was one of those foods that had to be chopped finely and snuck into birdie breads. One day, I offered him Broccoli Potato Casserole baby food on a spoon and he couldn't gulp it down fast enough. I keep meaning to puree some fresh broccoli with some freshly steamed potato to see if he'd like that. He should, but you just never know with him.

But, I did get a chance to experiment with the Peas & Carrots baby food. After reaching for a baby food to feed to Pickles, and noticing that the sole ingredients were peas and carrots, I realized that I had both so I steamed them, finely diced them and offered them to Pickles on a spoon. He turned his nose up at it, couldn't even be bothered to send it flying. Hmmmmmm, I wonder if he'll eat the baby food. I opened up the jar of Peas & Carrots baby food, offered it to Pickles and he lapped it up. He almost fell over front wards when I snatched the spoon away and ran to the kitchen to puree the veggies I had just cooked for him. When I was done, I returned to offer him the fresh stuff. He balked at first, touched it gingerly with his tongue, took a small scoop then larger and larger mouthfuls as he stared up at me with a look that seemed to say, *Well played, Mother. Well played.*

I should interject here and explain about the baby food. Pickles has always loved mushies, especially warm, on a spoon. It's left over from weaning but it's also a great bonding time for us. I don't actually eat what he's eating but I pretend to, and that makes Pickles happy. He likes to share and will actually stop eating off the spoon and wait for you to take some when he feels it's time for your share.

Some people think a parrot should be weaned within 3 or 6 months but I say there's no set time for it and, as a matter of fact, let it go on forever. I liken it to humans with milk. We drank it as babies but continued to drink it our whole lives. It's delicious, it's good for us and it gives us comfort so why would we wean ourselves off it? If something gives a parrot happiness and comfort, why take it away from them?

I've always spoon fed him but it was difficult finding nutritious things to feed him, until I looked at baby food jars and realized it's pure nutrition for birds, not just human babies. Pickles really enjoys them (especially the mixed vegetables) and, since he's not crazy about very many types of fruit, it's a healthy way to get different kinds of fruits into him. I've started making our own purees but it's not always practical because of the seasons and also, it can be difficult to preserve in any sort of quantities. So, it's a healthy alternative for the times you can't make it yourself.

You never want to offer him something other than what he has asked for. That's an unforgivable offense. He once asked me for potato but I had none cooked so I handed him something I thought he'd like better – a piece of banana. I don't know, maybe it was a shock to the taste buds and he wasn't expecting something sweet so he had to use my skin and blood for a palate cleanser.

I found out that onions aren't the only food that makes you cry when I got hit in the eyeball with a macadamia nut I tried to pass off as an almond when we were out of them. And, another time almost had my eyeball replaced by a grape because it was cold from the fridge and he only likes them room temperature.

He noticed some banana bread that I had baked and left on the counter and, had he bothered to ask, would have found out – before he sneaked onto the counter, jumped on the rim, flipped it off its trivet and scared himself half to death – that it was actually a birdie bread for him and no sneaking was required.

I had to chuckle one day when Neil fed Pickles his supper and then proceeded to give fresh water to both Pickles and Neeka Dog. I watched as Neil walked into the livingroom with the dog's water bowl and stood in front

31

of the cage with a confused look on his face. Pickles removed his head from his supper dish and stood staring up at Neil, also with a confused look on his face, as if to say, *Yeah, it doesn't look right to me either.* Neil finally snapped out of it, walked back to the kitchen to place the water on the floor and fetch a bowl for Pickles when suddenly, Pickles realized he didn't have any fresh water. It was like a 'Got Milk?' moment. Pickles was panicking because he ALWAYS gets fresh water immediately after being handed his supper and almost always pauses while eating long enough to remind us, "Fresh water?" just in case we might forget. Most times, he takes a few bites then walks across his perch for a water chaser before continuing with his supper. So, suddenly he gets it in his head that he's very thirsty – no, he decided he was literally DYING of thirst and screaming, "Fresh water, fresh water!" while Neil ran as quickly as he could, in a panic to please Pickles.

He's also lazy. Pickles doesn't like to work too hard for food. He has all kinds of foraging toys, mostly designed to make a bird solve a puzzle to release a treat. It's hard to say how good he is at these puzzles because he never seems motivated enough to try very hard. And it's not like I'm going to starve him to get him to work harder. He has often solved the puzzles but he'd rather bag at me for hours, hollering for a snack, than work for it however, I have been getting more and more creative at making my own foraging items which he seems to prefer.

He's too lazy to use his beak to crack the shell on an almond – one of his favorite foods of all times – so we have to make sure that they're kind of chipped so he has an easy place to start. The same with a walnut. No way we can hand him a walnut without one quarter of the shell snapped off so he can reach the meat inside. From there, he will worry his beak around inside to get every crumb and drop it to the floor or cage bottom when he's done. And yet! ... later on, out of shear boredom, he will climb down to retrieve the shell and then chew the entire thing up until there's nothing left but dust! For the longest time, I just thought he had a weak or sensitive beak.

One day, Mr. Fussy is on the back of the couch and spots what looks like a raisin just laying there on the windowsill. He put it in his mouth, rolled it around on his tongue, realized it was a dead fly and since he doesn't like dead flies, he spit it out. He likes raisins even less than flies so I don't know why he put it in his mouth to begin with.

But, food can be fun too. I don't know how he managed to do it but one day, I did a double take when he had noodles atop his head, looking a little Rastafarian. And, if you are sitting on the counter and, if you yell 'peek-a-boo' long enough and loud enough, toast might appear. Toast likes that game.

*I had climbed down from my cage and was investigating in the kitchen, behind Mom's back, while she was doing the dishes. I noticed Neeka Dog eating something out of a big green bowl on the floor so I waddled over and found bigger pellets than mine and was about to have a taste testing but apparently you can't sample someone's food without them tattling to your mother.*

## A Bad Thing Turned Good

Pickles was standing on top of a bell that was tied on a rope and attached to other ropes above. I knew he was in for a bit of a shock as I watched him

33

busily chewing through the rope the bell was hanging on. Sure enough, there he was, hanging by a tiny strand and just as he reached to finish the job, the strand gave out and Pickles fell to the floor with a squawk. He managed to land on his feet and for a moment he stood in shock but quickly recovered and realized that a bad occurrence had somehow worked out in his favor so he took off running like a chicken with his head cut off. He wanted to beat it out of there before I could stop him and since Daddy was in the bathroom, he headed down the hall as fast as his feet could carry him.

Neil was just coming out the door as Pickles arrived so he picked him up and set him on the bed while he changed his clothes. Neeka the Dog, not wanting to be left out, jumped up on the bed and scared Pickles who had been standing with his back to Neeka. Pickles was angry at being startled and turned to yell at Neeka to "Get back up!" Even though Pickles was a little mixed up with his command and may have said it wrong, everybody knew what he meant and Neeka jumped down off the bed.

I had been holding the phone and about to make a call when suddenly it rang. Since Pickles always says, "Hello" in the background after the phone rings, I figured I'd hold it up to his face so he could actually answer the phone this time but instead of the usual 'hello', he opted for the sound of a fart. I snatched it away and said 'hello' into the receiver, hoping the caller didn't think I had actually farted into the phone myself before answering it and also hoping that the person at the other end would know I'm not that sort of person. It was never mentioned and it turned out it was someone requesting that Pickles and I come to their school for a class presentation. I figured I would explain it when I went and everyone would get a good laugh but as it turned out, the presentation was cancelled. Perhaps they didn't want a farter in class.

*Mom – I just got back from a dangerous safari! Pickles, by 'dangerous safari' does that mean you climbed down from your cage, walked down the hall and had the crap scared out of you when the furnace kicked in? No it doesn't, Mom! – But in this case, yes.*

## A Bouquet of Feathers

As Pickles' fans all know, Pickles is afraid of feathers. Just doesn't make sense, does it. I keep saying he suffers from pteronophobia; the fear of being tickled by feathers but thinks it's only the loose ones that are dangerous, not the ones stuck to his body. One feather is usually okay and like many birds, he will use the end of the shaft to scratch his head – but usually only if it has come loose in his own talon. If you try to hand him a feather, he gets angry or tries to back away from it. He's especially afraid of my pink feather dusters and unfortunately for him, I have enough to last more than a lifetime because I found them for about 25 cents each at a swap meet. It's not like he's terrified of them, he just doesn't like it if one gets too close to him.

Every time Pickles molts feathers, I pick them up and save them in a large jar. For years I have given them to a Native Indian friend of mine but lately I've been putting one in books for people who order a book straight from me for the first time. Just the first book because I'd never have enough feathers for every single book that's ordered from me. I read somewhere about someone tying a bunch of feathers together and hanging them for their parrot, that it makes a good preening toy so they don't over preen

35

themselves, so that's what I did – built a bouquet of feathers for Pickles and hung it on top of his cage, totally forgetting about his fear of feathers.

I had built it and hung it without thinking while Pickles was hanging with his Daddy in the diningroom and then I forgot about it. Later, Neil took Pickles home to his cage and when he went to set him on the top, Pickles freaked and flew out of the room. Of course, Neil had no idea why he did that so he kept going to get him and kept trying to set him down on the cage top but Pickles would have none of that! Finally, all the commotion caught my attention and I went to see what the deal was, and then I felt bad.

I moved the bouquet to the back corner of the cage and Pickles was fine with that so I left them for him to get used to and hopefully start chewing on. I meant to move them because they were directly above his favorite night perch inside the cage but completely forgot when Pickles went to bed and got covered up but everything went fine and it didn't bother him so they remained, even though they sat untouched, for days if not weeks.

One morning I uncovered Pickles and reached inside the cage to change his water dish and I froze. Blood and carnage everywhere! Pickles had been plucking some chest feathers but among the plucked fluffies were flight feathers mixed with blood. I glanced up at Pickles and he seemed fine and there was no blood on him so I inspected things closer and finally realized that the blood was red poop – a result of raspberries for his supper the night before – and the feathers were the bouquet that he had managed to pull through the bars and separate from the bouquet. I shouldn't have told Neil; it would have been cool to set it up again for him to find and freak out over one morning.

*Mom, why did you put this icky piece of cantaloupe on my skewer of fruit and veggies? Because it's good, Pickles. Hey, you're right, Mom – it looks good stuck to that painting.*

## A Life of Poop

When did poop take over my life? It's been so gradual but then suddenly I find that that's almost all I talk about. At what point did I start dominating all conversation around family and friends with the subject of poop – helpful poop information, stories about poop – you know, just all the pooping that goes on in one's house. Somehow, I feel the need to spread the word and inform. At what point did it stop disgusting me, start entertaining me and convince me than everyone within shouting distance, must surely want me to share. I'm not kidding about shouting distance. I once found myself floating on the lake in my float tube and telling a poop story to an acquaintance fisherman anchored about 50 feet away from me. Naturally, the conversation turned to Pickles and poop and I later realized that, by the way sound travels on calm water; I had transmitted my story to all on land and lake.

With winter upon us - hunkered down in the house, avoiding the cold and snow and all of us suffering cabin fever - poop seems a little more in-your-face these days. I think Pickles is not only getting sick of us but he's also getting bored with no access to his outside aviary. He doesn't fly off or wander around on the floor much; it just seems like it because he usually gets into some kind of trouble when he does so I write about it. Regardless, one day he was particularly ticked off with everyone and everything and when he gets like that he starts squawking, leaning low and flapping his wings in frustration. He got the wings going pretty hard and before he knew it, he was taking off. He flew through the livingroom, kitchen, down the hall and landed on the bedroom floor.

He usually takes a poop before he travels but he hadn't expected lift-off so he didn't get his chance until he landed. When I got there, he wouldn't step up on my hand. He squawked at me while avoiding my hand and running to and fro – through his poop – because he was cornered with nowhere to run except through it. Stupid me. When I finally got him up on my hand, I was rewarded with nice track marks on my hands and cuffs, and now I couldn't get him off me. He refused to step down and each time I tried, his talons dug deeper – sharp talons as a result of temporarily removing his sand perch.

I was in excruciating pain and I knew the only place he might step down at this point, was the couch. He loves the couch and the window to the outside so he happily stepped down, expecting me to sit and play with him. I didn't have time though, and I wasn't about to reward him for taking his little unauthorized expedition, so I shut the screen door between the livingroom and kitchen, walked out and left him alone on the couch. He doesn't like being alone on the couch so, as expected, he climbed down, waddled to his cage and climbed back up to where he started off to begin with, while I washed and disinfected my poopy scratches and talon holes. (The screen door was put there to keep Pickles contained, and not running around the house, if we need to go out. Pickles is only caged when he asks to go to bed at night)

Later on, I went into the livingroom, took Pickles down for a brief play period on the back of the couch and then set him back on his cage. I was sitting on the couch, reading a book, and absent-mindedly reached over to stroke Neeka Dog's back only to smear a big, gooey mess of Pickles' poop the length of his body. I hadn't noticed Neeka foraging beneath Pickles' playstand and Pickles had obviously hit his mark from above – it had landed between Neeka's shoulder blades, where he was unable to reach it. Nice, more poop on my hand.

Later on still, Neil took the couch for a quick afternoon nap. His head no sooner hit the couch pillow when he shot right back up, swearing a blue streak. Yup, Pickles had planted a steaming pile right where Neil's ear could meet up with it. I felt kind of bad because I hadn't noticed Pickles doing it earlier (I was a little preoccupied with TV) but I couldn't help but burst out laughing at the look on his face and his pretty ear. Pickles enjoys a good laugh too so when I started laughing, so did he. Neil didn't.

At some point after that, Pickles had decided to fly to the back of the couch so he could watch any outdoor activities going on with the wild birds or neighbours. He did this while we were busy in the other rooms but we knew he had flown down there and we kept our eyes on him from afar. A short time later, I heard his wings flapping and knew he had flown back to his cage top so I went to check for any poop droppings on the couch. He hadn't pooped on the cushions but I noticed a couple of poops on the floor and went to get a tissue to clean it up but by the time I returned, Neeka had cleaned it up for me. Totally disgusting, but also convenient sometimes. Gag.

That's four in one day, you'd think that'd be enough but Neeka poops too, you know. Poor thing; for a 6-pound Min Pin with hardly any coat of hair, going outside in winter can be quite challenging for him at times. We had hit

–29 Celsius the past couple of days and the snow on the ground was crystallizing, cold as heck and rough on Neeka's paw pads. Ever see a dog trying to keep all four feet of the ground while trying to take a crap? He did manage three at one point, but only briefly.

I changed things around in his cage a bit and moved a perch and bowl set-up. Since I did, I was finding poop in his supper bowl in the morning (we leave his supper in his cage all night because we live in a very arid climate and nothing gets mouldy so it's safer to leave most of his foods out for longer periods than most people can) so I eventually moved the bowl over since he was obviously perching above it at night. After I moved it, I was still finding poop in the dish in the morning. The bugger was obviously aiming for the bowl because there was never any poop on the paper below the dish.

And then there's those fun mornings when we uncover Pickles to find what we think is blood on the cage paper having forgotten that he ate raspberries, beets, cherries or something else that turned his poop red in the night.

So, yeah - poop. Can't live with it, can't live without.

*Mom, while you were on the phone, I ate all the raisins. What raisins, Pickles? The ones you scattered all over the windowsill for me, Mom. We don't have any raisins, Pickles. Not anymore, Mom, cuz I ate them all. Pickles, those weren't raisins. Gack!*

# Alien

Pickles' stainless steel talon bucket, which hangs on his favorite roosting perch inside the cage, was starting to come loose so Neil grabbed a pair of pliers and went to fix it. Neil has to reach way inside the cage to secure the bucket while his other hand is outside tightening it up which means his chin is resting on the top of the cage while his whole body is forced up against the bars, leaving him vulnerable and fair game to Pickles. He scrambles across the top of the cage like a spider and stands on the top, (face to face) eyeball to eyeball with Neil then goes for the eyeglasses, yanking them off Daddy's head. Neil is frozen in place like some macabre scary movie with the character paralysed and forced to watch whatever evil befalls him. Pickles stands before him, glasses in one talon, waving them around with an In-Your-Face kinda attitude – taking full advantage of Neil's predicament.

I come to the rescue and confiscate the glasses so he heads down the cage and sits on the edge of the playstand where he can watch Daddy, just inches away. He's intrigued by the pliers going up and down, up and down as Neil is screwing the bolt on the outside of the cage and decides to test a handle as it comes toward him so he grabs onto it with his beak. At the moment he latches on, Neil is entering the upswing so Pickles goes with it.

Now Pickles and the pliers are right next to the cage bars so Pickles can easily grab the bars with his talons but he doesn't. He just hangs by his beak, feet straight below him and rides the plier handles up and down – honking like a goose. He enjoyed the ride for the duration of the screwing and once Neil was finished, Pickles was intent on finding out what new toys were in his talon bucket so he ordered, "Lights off" as he hastened into his cage. I

41

threw his night time almond into the bucket, closed the cage and covered it as he whistled his happy song.

Later in the evening, after watching a rather spooky movie, Neil was making snacks in the kitchen while I stared blankly at the TV screen. I caught a movement at the corner of my eye in Pickles' general direction but when I turned to look, I saw nothing. I returned my gaze to the screen and a few moments later, something moved just out of my vision again so once again, I turned my head to catch the movement and there it was – a small, moving mound beneath the cage sheet, slithering up the side of the cage between the sheet and the bars. I panicked for Pickles! What WAS this and was it after him?? I knew I should make a dash to save him but I was frozen in place, in momentary terror as the lumpy entity writhed around the cage. Motherly instincts, my ass.

After a few moments I had to ask myself why Pickles wasn't freaking out and flapping all over his cage and thought ... no way – that can't be HIM, can it? Just then, Neil walked in and I pointed to the creeping lump of sheet. I thought his eyes would pop out of his head as he stood stock-still, rooted to the floor in shock. With Neil at my back to cover me, I walked to the cage and slowly lifted the sheet. I half expected some kind of alien and half expected it to be Pickles but either way, I dropped the sheet and screamed like a little girl when just as it was appearing, it belched a ghastly sound! A moment after I dropped the cover I realized, in hindsight, that I had glimpsed a red tail so gingerly picked it up and peeked again. It was hideous! Beady yellow eyes rose up from the darkness, embedded in a bobbing head of glee and accompanied by snickers and nose laughs. Yes, twas Pickles. Pickles had unlatched the cage door or I had forgot to latch it and Pickles saw an opportunity for some totally cool and different adventure. Either way, Neil and I felt pretty stupid.

*OMG OMG OMG - I'm melting, Mom! Oh, good grief Pickles, you are NOT melting – water won't kill you. No, Mom, I'm pretty sure the water is acid and it's eating me up! Stop being silly and take your bath, Pickles! False alarm, Mom ... that's not melted body parts, it's just my poop in the water. Scary.*

## Angry Butt Bird

I took Neeka Dog for a nice long walk around the lake and when I returned I fell, exhausted, face down on the couch without acknowledging Pickles. Pickles expects a greeting and quick recap of my outing and when he realized it wasn't forthcoming, he decided to join me on the couch instead. A quick flap and he went from his playstand to my butt and refused to budge from there when I reached around to my backside to get him to step up on my hand. I thought that if I just ignored him, he might climb up the back of the couch but he continued using my ample butt for a perch.

I didn't dare ignore him much longer for fear I'd fall asleep and leave him to find trouble somewhere so I hauled by aching body up to back up onto the floor and stand. Pickles hung like a woodpecker to a tree trunk and still refused to step up when I reached around for him. I couldn't see him but I could feel his head rubbing against my fingers as he asked for a "scratch". Guess he was trying to get in on some 'butt scratch' action.

No way he was moving and any more attempts on my part just prompted nose laughs and head bobs from Pickles so I walked through the house with the little butt cling-on hanging upside down, chattering to himself. I opened the linen closet knowing that he couldn't resist that and I was correct but now I had merely exchanged one problem for another – the task of removing him from the closet.

No amount of coaxing or bribing was going to get him out of there but I really needed to lie down so finally, I closed the door and laid down on the floor where I could listen for him chewing on wood or squawking to get out. I knew he would just fall asleep in the dark, because he'd done it before, so I kind of dosed for a few minutes until I was rested.

When I stood back up and opened the closet, there was Pickles in the very same spot and so sleepy and comfy on a fluffy towel that he could barely open his eyes to look at me. I used this opportunity to have him step up before he knew what was happening and I took him back and set him on top of his cage.

This infuriated him when he realized he'd been duped and he immediately headed for his outside pellet bowl, stood on the rim, stuck his beak inside, vibrated his head and angrily scattered all the pellets out of the bowl and into the air all around him.

Talk about a pain in the butt.

*When you're going up a stair, with your mom following right behind you, just as she takes a step, change your mind and go back down. Moms look*

44

*really funny spread-eagle and humped over on all fours trying not to fall on you.*

## Apples

If you've read my previous books, you know that I make my own birdie breads for Pickles. He's always been a fussy eater and rejected most fruits and vegetables so, to get all the nutrients into his fussy little body, I very finely chop up the ones he won't eat and bake it in a birdie bread with other things he does like. It's not as good as fresh fruits and veggies but it helps a lot.

I always felt that by doing this, he might acquire a taste for some things and I think it might have worked, although I know parrots also change their minds for no apparent reason when it comes to food. It may be because it's from a different grower, different area, different season, a little riper or maybe not as ripe. At the time of this writing, Pickles has started eating a lot more things than he used to. Among other things, he's decided he LOVES rutabagas and he can't seem to get enough leafy greens whether it's beet greens, lettuce or spinach (spinach is limited because it blocks/absorbs calcium) but apples have become his very favorite. This is great because they are a lot lower in sugar than his previous favorites, grapes and bananas. I also like it when berries are in season because he likes blackberries and raspberries, which are even lower in sugar.

A friend gave us a large quantity of apples this past year so we decided to process most of them by canning them. That meant peeling, coring and chopping so that's what I was doing when Pickles decided to join me as I sat working at the kitchen table. He seldom flies, even though he is hardly ever clipped, and prefers to walk to wherever he wants to go and we discourage him from doing so but this time he was bent on flying as he was in a hurry to get near all those apples. He's a good flyer and very accurate at landing (I can hold up a finger and he will land on it with no problem) but in his excitement, he over shot my shoulder and landed on the floor a few feet away. He may think he can soar like an eagle but he creeps like a rat and this rat, once he climbed up my pants, my shirt and onto my shoulder announced loudly in my ear, "APPLE SNACKERY, DAMMIT".

I put him down on the table and let him go at it and eat his fill while I worked, careful to keep him away from any toxic apple seeds, and he had a great time running around eating and tossing everything in sight. But we won't tell those people who we've shared our apples with in the form of pie, crisps and applesauce. No, it's our little secret.

*Oh, such a glorious day. Sitting in the aviary, first in the warm sunshine, then in the cool shade. Dipping me feet and beak into the cool water in me birdbath then preening and napping in the gentle breeze. Watching the trout cruising peacefully in the pond while the wild birdies frolic in the yard and bathe in the gurgling waterfall. I copy the sparrows and start a friendly conversation with them. I chirp louder though because I am further away and soon I decide that perhaps they can't hear me well enough from across the pond and as I stick my head into my stainless steel bucket to chirp as loud as I can, I'm thinking what a perfect, beautiful day it is. And then I think - Good God, I've made myself deaf again.*

Babysitting

Neil was laying laminate floor in the house so I had to baby sit and entertain Pickles most of the day to keep Pickles from trying to 'help' him and that meant keeping him out of whatever room Neil was working on at the time. Pickles is used to having us taxi him to whatever room he wants to be and doesn't like staying in one place more than an hour or so at a time. He also doesn't like being alone in a room for too long either so that meant I had to give up most of my own work for the day to keep him company.

Neil was only part way through laminating the livingroom before Pickles starting accompanying him with the snapping sounds from snapping one piece of laminate into another. Pickles quite enjoyed this and sometimes made it a race between the two of them by snapping faster than Daddy. While this kept him entertained for a while I did the dishes and washed some of his talon toys.

I was another source of entertainment for him as he laid in ambush among his kitchen/diningroom ropes waiting for opportunities to bonk me on the head as I walked between the two rooms picking up dishes and toys. I had changed some rope positions and placed one of them too close to unsuspecting pedestrians. I knew better than to walk too close but I kept getting preoccupied and forgetting about it. Pickles can bonk really hard so it's a wonder I didn't lose an eye. Sometimes, living with Pickles can be like living with Dennis the Menace except without the laughs.

To protect myself until I could get around to switching the ropes so he couldn't reach people walking by, I set him on the counter to play with some talon toys and watch me do the dishes but he was more interested in getting to the drying dishes on the other side and kept scooting along the edge of the counter and under my arms. He usually did it slow enough that I could wipe my hands before I grabbed him and put him back but the last time, he made a mad dash and I ended up grabbing him with my hands full of suds. He wasn't happy about that because now he had to sit with his butt hanging off the counter, cleaning all the soap off with his beak. But at least it kept him busy long enough for me to finish.

I drained the sink water and placed some pieces of nutriberry and walnuts on the counter for Pickles to cleanse his pallet of soapsuds. After a couple of munches, he jumped in the sink, cocked his head to look down the drain and then dropped a piece of walnut inside. He stood staring down the hole then jumped back on the counter, took a pine nut, jumped back in the sink and dropped it down the hole too. Then he started to regurge for the drain but instead of dropping it down the hole, he shook his head and got it all over the place – including the nice clean dishes. I don't know what he saw down there but whatever it was, Pickles figured it was hungry and needed to be fed.

It was time to move him so I could move on to do other things but Pickles hadn't spent enough time yet on his beloved counter and refused to step up. As soon as I offered him my hand, he'd run away but as soon as I put my hand back down to my side, he would run back to the edge of the counter, look up at me sweetly, raise his talon and say, "Step up" but the moment I offered my hand again, he would run away laughing. When I told him he was being a brat, he answered in typical teenage style, "Whatever". I find it amazing the parrots understand teasing, at least Pickles' sure does. And, I hate to admit it but he's obviously picked up 'whatever' from me and my snotty attitude. I finally got him to step up by offering him a piece of banana and took him back to his ropes to eat it.

Once back on his ropes, he was content to hang around and play music with a big bell but he soon discovered that I had another poorly placed rope that he could reach the doorframe from. When I finally glanced up to catch him putting his signature on the edges and hollered at him to stop, he laughed and laughed and laughed until finally I had to laugh too. As soon as I did, he went back to chewing the doorframe. Little bugger. Laughing to distract me into forgetting all about it – smart.

Neil soon finished the flooring in the livingroom and moved on to the kitchen so I took Pickles back and set him on top of his cage with a piece of carrot. The phone rang and I could see by the number in my call display that it was those bloody telemarketers that kept calling to say there's a problem with my computer and offering to fix it. It's a scam but they wouldn't stop calling so I hit the answer button, held it up to Pickles and let him say, "Hello" then I set it just out of reach and left it for him to chat with the telemarketers. I don't know what was going on at the other end of the line but Pickles talked up a storm on this end. I continued to do this every time they called, if I bothered to answer it at all, and eventually the telemarketers stopped calling.

*There's some kinds of veggies that I don't like and while Dad was chopping and dicing veggies for their supper, he would hand me a piece of whatever he was chopping. It was the icky stuff though so I would just grab it with my beak and toss it to the dog. After awhile I noticed all the nice neat piles of delicious looking veggies on Dad's cutting board so I started running over, grabbing a piece of something then running back to my side of the counter to eat it. Dad called me a goof and said it was all stuff that I swore I didn't like and that piece of ginger I snatched was the same thing he had tried to offer to me earlier and I wouldn't eat it. I call BULL and say he was just hoarding all the good stuff. He says I only liked everything because it was stolen. I'll just let him think what he likes.*

## Christmas Decorating

I grabbed the can of spray snow and headed for the livingroom windows with full intentions of finishing the Christmas decorating but the big, fluffy snow flakes coming down outside, adding to the 2 or 3 feet of fresh, white snow on the ground just made me want to curl up under a blanket on the couch and read a book, so that's what I did.

After a few minutes, Pickles insisted on joining me and since I was using my Ereader, instead of a paper book, I decided he could be trusted to behave and stay away from my book. He was okay for a few minutes but then he decided he wanted attention so he tried ripping the Ereader from my hands so I grabbed the small throw blanket off the rocking chair next to me and threw it on top of Pickles in hopes that he would play 'fort' and leave me alone for awhile. It worked. Pickles decided to lay still under the blanket so I went back to reading.

After awhile, I had forgotten about him because he had been so quiet so I glanced in his direction and there he was, head sticking out of a hole he had chewed in the blanket. He just sat there, happy and content with his work and the lovely cape that he had created. He looked up at me with sweet, sleepy eyes and cooed his pleasure and comfort so I didn't have the heart to get upset with him. Besides, I have no shortage of throw blankets.

I watched as Pickles' eyes started to droop then close. Neeka the Dog was curled at my feet, grooming his feet with sleepy eyes and between watching him groom himself (which always makes me sleepy, as well as watching Pickles preen) and watching Pickles doze, my eyes got heavy and I fell into a light doze myself. Of course, this was just a ploy of Pickles to make me drop my guard and close my eyes long enough for him to pull out the TV guide from between the cushions and get to work on it. That ended quiet time so off to snow paint the windows.

I pulled the couch out far enough from the two windows so that Pickles couldn't try to eat the snow as I sprayed it but he was more interested in the actual can, rather than what was coming out of it. He seemed really interested in the sound effects from the metal ball inside whenever I shook it, trying to squeeze out the last of the can, and ran back and forth along the back of the couch, doing the wing splaying and little squeaks and 'uh, uh, uh's' that he does when he gets amorous. Pretty soon, he started to regurgitate.

I didn't think much about it at first but then I started to worry when he kept it up and just as I noticed the whopping amount of bright red mixture in his mouth (a nice blend of Mountain Ash berries and Currants), he began to shake his head. I dove for him, in what seemed like slow motion, in an attempt to sweep him off the couch but by the time I reached him, gurge was spraying like stucco from his mouth and adhering to the nice white snow on the windows.

As I stood there, inspecting his artwork, his head vibrated once more as he shot another round. The red mixed in quite nicely and Christmassy with the white snow and if you didn't know what it was, you might think it quite lovely. There wasn't enough snow left in the can to cover it over and since I wouldn't be making another trip all the way into Kamloops to get some more before Christmas (which was two days away), I had two choices – wash all the snow off the windows or leave it. I opted to leave it. I mean, who would notice?

*I'm bored; take me to my dining room ropes. I'm not happy here; take me home. I'm not happy here; take me to play on the freezer. I'm not happy here; take me outside to my aviary. I'm not happy here; take me home. I'm not ... jeez, what's the matter with you, Mom? Why are you getting so cranky? God, you can be so difficult at times.*

<u>Coffee Time</u>

I was sitting in the living room, having my coffee, when I noticed there was a hanging toy with poop all over it, hanging on Pickles' playstand. I decided it was time to change some toys anyway so I grabbed a box of clean ones and stood in front of the playstand, drinking my coffee and thinking about where to put the new ones. Once I had it figured out, I set my coffee mug down on the base of the stand while I got to work.

Pickles loves it when I hang toys or clean the stand so he got right in there to help by hanging off each one or grabbing them with his beak as I clipped them on. He's a real gabber while we're doing this so we talk back and forth as we work.

When I finished, I grabbed the dirty toys and went to put them away, forgetting about my mug of coffee. I returned just in time to grab it as Pickles was reaching for it. He won't drink coffee but he would have had fun dumping the mug and he squawked his disappointment as I headed to my rocking chair to finish drinking it.

Just as I was about to sip the last of it, I happened to look inside my mug and what I saw, sent me gagging and running to the kitchen sink. Whether it was on purpose or a convenient accident, Pickles must have managed a bull's-eye from his perch above. I don't think he's aware enough to know I would be drinking it and if he was, I'm sure he'd think it's just an added bonus, but I don't doubt for a moment that he deliberately took aim, fired and watched it drop with accuracy into my cup.

*Mom, I've prepared some of your favorite foods for you - banana, almonds, grapes, potato and cheerios. And for your convenience, all regurgitated together in one nice gooey lump.*

# Color My World

We do a lot of painting around the house, or at least Neil does. I choose the colors, he does the labor. I'm not very good at picking out paint. I know what I want, it just looks different once it's up on our walls, hence the reason why we're always painting around here. I really hate it though when you're stuck between mistakes, too busy to repaint and you can't stop people from seeing it so they think you really suck at decorating. You get so used to it yourself that sometimes you don't even think about explaining the gaudy walls to guests.

It's great for us bird people these days because gone are the days when you had to wait for warm weather so that you could open windows and move your bird to another room, away from the toxic fumes. For a while, you could buy low VOC paint but now you can buy quality paint with *NO* VOC whatsoever. So now you can paint all you want without removing your parrot from the room. Well, unless it's Pickles.

Neil was painting the livingroom while Pickles and he chatted. Pickles loves to chat while you work at housework or renovations and that's why the sudden silence should have been a clue for Neil to do a shoulder check. Instead, Neil kept replacing the paint on his roller from the roller tray next to him. A funny sounding, 'hellllllloooooo' finally gave him pause so he turned to find Pickles on the rim of the Naucho Yellow paint can, leaning far forward, butt up in the air, trying to reach the paint near the bottom while enjoying the cool echo the almost empty tin can made. Why Neil didn't lay the lid on top, until he needed it again, I don't know and Neil was rueing it as he swept him up and ran for the kitchen sink where he quickly filled it to birdy belly depth and plunged him in to rinse the thick coat of paint off his talons.

No way was Pickles expecting something like this! To be dumped without warning into WATER, when he'd likely prefer boiling oil, was just beyond his comprehension and so the shock really aided in buying time to wipe off his feet before he came to his senses and bit the crap out of Neil. Fast as he could, Neil got him rinsed off and plunked back down on his playstand. What he failed to notice, is that Pickles had touched his cheek with a painted talon and now had three Naucho Yellow dots that would take over 7 months to completely fade.

Now I had something else to explain when people asked why he had paint on his face. *Why, he loves paint – It's his favorite toy – we give it to him all the time!* I mean, I may as well say that. I think people stopped believing anything I say, quite some time ago.

I wasn't home that day and Neil actually had to quit painting because he couldn't keep Pickles from climbing down his cage and bolting for the paint can. He never even thought about locking Pickles in his cage because we forget that cages can be locked in the daytime, not just at night. We never lock him in, even when we leave the house, so it doesn't occur to us to put him inside to get something done. Instead, we wait for a more convenient time. He has trained us well.

Sometime, in the next few days, Neil managed to finish painting the livingroom. He cleaned everything up but missed a paintbrush on the floor. I happened to walk into the livingroom at some point, just in time to catch

Neeka standing over it. When I hollered at him to get away from it he poked his dick, as he always does when he's in trouble, so I had no reason to believe it wasn't him until I picked up the brush and saw a couple of beak marks. I don't know why I fell for it because Neeka never chews on anything but his own toys so this would have been a first, but if Pickles had a plan, it almost worked.

Pickles almost managed another tattoo when he flew to the back of the couch to talk to all the birdies out the window. Neil had pulled the couch out so that it didn't get paint off the wall and had left enough of a gap for Pickles to disappear when he miscalculated his landing. He fell like a brick to the floor, sliding down the wall, and luckily the paint had dried enough for it to stay put but the room was finished and we took all the paint toys and fun rides away for good.

*You may think I'm 'just' a bird but to the ants in our house, I am Food God.*

## Counting

I've never really worked with Pickles to teach him how to count but I really should because he gets some weird kind of kick out of it. Whenever he's sitting on the kitchen counter while I'm preparing his supper, I put it in the microwave and count out loud to 20 because my microwave doesn't have a second timer, only a dial that doesn't accurately show the seconds. As I count, Pickles dances and bobs his head to the counting as if it's a really good song.

One day I was counting and right after saying 'three' and just before I could say 'four', Pickles hollered, "Last snack!" The little goof thinks that is what comes after 'three' because we often offer him four pine nut snacks as a rewards and we let him know when we're going to take the snack bowl away by counting out the three snacks as he takes them and then telling him, "Last snack". Often he gets sneaky about it and when we tell him 'last snack', he uses his lower mandible to scoop a large mouthful.

(You can see a video of Pickles dancing to the counting on You Tube under 'Pickles The Parrot Dances to Counting')

*Neeka the Dog is so silly. He has to follow mom everywhere and if he doesn't make it to the bathroom with her fast enough, she closes the door on him so he has to wait in the hallway. He gets all upset as if maybe there's a secret door in the bathroom that mom can escape through. Neeka's afraid she'll disappear and I'm afraid she won't.*

## Perfect Perches

Every now and then I come across some well-meaning article about perch sizes. They will usually include a formula for determining the correct sizes for different sized birds and explain how the wrong size can cause arthritis and general discomfort. It makes complete sense, in theory, but I have to wonder if the authors of these articles actually have parrots of their own.

In the early days, Neil and I spent a lot of time researching perch sizes, perch materials, proper placement etc. and it was all for nothing. Pickles always chooses to sit in the most unlikely spots such as the very thin rims of his food and water bowls, the skinny square bars at the top of his cage, really fat ropes, the skinny edge of his foraging tray, the thin edge of his Fun Factory ball opening, the flat base of his playstand and his big, round coconut man etc. We seldom find him perched on the recommended and ergonomically sized branches. Even when he's sleeping at night, most of his sleep time is spent on his ceramic bowl. I think the trick is to provide a variety of sizes and let them choose their favorites the same as they would in the wild.

We like to make perches out tree branches and usually choose the ones that are fairly easy for him to chew and we always leave the bark on them – Pickles loves peeling that off. We get most of our branches from our own yard and then wash and sterilize them. We use the wood that is non-toxic to parrots plus we know they are safe from pesticides because we don't use it.

As most people know, Neil builds playstands for Pickles and sometimes we use softer types of wood to make a stand that is specifically for chewing and destroying – usually Poplar branches. We had one stand that contained a soft wood branch that Pickles particularly liked to use. It extended off by itself and made a nice perching spot and it was ergonomically too skinny for him so his talons wrapped right around the branch. He used a section that was about 10 inches from the end for rubbing and conditioning his beak and it was wearing very thin. He used the very end of the branch to bite little chunks off to chew as gum and for whittling into a nice sharp point.

That nice, sharp point stabbed me in the arm one day while I was cleaning the stand with a big bowl of water. It got me good and it really hurt – enough for me to holler and swear in surprise. Pickles had been hanging upside down on a branch next to the sharp one so that he could bonk me in the head if the chance arose. As soon as I hollered, he righted himself and scampered over to the sharp branch, laughing and head bobbing the whole way. He didn't get to bonk me in the head but my reaction was the same as if he did so he thought this was just dandy. He reached the end of the branch to sit and continue his laughter just as the branch snapped off in the beak conditioning spot, carrying him straight down and into my bowl of water. His laughter turned to anger at getting wet. Falls are fine, even fun, but water ruins everything – but not for me. It made me forget my pain and now it was my turn to laugh and head bob.

*I told Mom I wanted some banana but she said there wasn't any. I couldn't believe it! I started beating up all my toys and throwing my pellets out of the bowl. Mom said, "Pickles! Don't be that way – don't be bitter!" "I'm not bitter, Mom. I'm just filled with disappointment and fury that has moved from my heart to my brain which is ready to explode with rage and kill everything and everybody in it's path if I don't get banana. Hey, where ya goin' in such a hurry?" "To the store, Pickles." "Oh, can you grab a banana while you're there?"*

# Darn Dog

Pickles was on the floor of his playstand, just walking around investigating stuff while I sat on the couch watching TV and eating a granola bar. When I got to the last of the bar, I threw it to Pickles to eat and it whizzed past his head and slid across the playstand floor. Pickles got angry about this – either because he thought I was throwing stuff at him, or because he had to chase after it instead of it landing neatly at his feet – so he ran after it and grabbed it in his beak to toss it away.

He does this all the time; grabs food that I give him, expecting it to be crap and ready to throw it in anger. But just as it is leaving his mouth, his tongue gets a taste of it and he realizes that it's not crap after all but it's too late to stop the momentum of the flinging crap. As soon as it flies, Pickles says "Ohhhhhhhh" in his whiney voice and wants it back, which I'm happy to oblige. However, when Pickles tossed it this time, Neeka Dog snatched it up and ate it. "Sorry Pickles, that was the last of it, there ain't no more," I told him.

He wasn't happy about this at all and stood on the edge of his playstand, glaring down at Neeka while Neeka sat staring back at him in hopes of more food. Finally, Pickles leaned way over and asked Neeka, "Do you wanna snack?" As Neeka sat politely, Pickles turned around and pooped him out a snack. I'm sure he meant it as an insult but that dog – he'll eat anything.

*Mom says I have an awful lot of FB friends but she wonders how many actually follow my page. She told me not to think I have a huge following or anything, that I'm not as popular as I might think. I don't know what she's*

*talking about because I happen to know that I am very popular among*
*women between 18 and 48 ... months left to serve in prison.*

## Feather Plucking Update

I spoke in previous books about the problem we were having with Pickles plucking his chest feathers. It's mainly just one spot on his chest and sometimes it's bare, other times he allows downy feathers to grow and then something gets him going again. Although there can be many causes for this, we always believed it was because he hates getting wet. We don't believe it is stress related because Pickles is an extremely happy and content bird. If it is diet related, we'll be darned if we can figure out what he's eating (or not eating) that could cause this. Pickles enjoys a pretty good diet, we offer him next to nothing in processed food and his diet continues to improve as he gets older and as he eats more fruits and veggies.

I took him down to his avian veterinarian in Vancouver back in the early spring of 2012 and he stayed for two nights while she conducted all the normal tests – blood panel, blood collection, bile acids, radiographs, gram stain etc. The only thing that indicated any problem that might cause the plucking was that he had some skin bacteria, which is understandable since he refuses to bathe and hates the spray bottle. (He will run around in a birdbath but only gets his feet and beak wet) We were given some Vetericyn VF Spray but when the bottle ran out, there was basically no change. Since the vet visit, we have made sure Pickles is sprayed with water two to three times a week, whether he likes it or not.

We were given a long list of things to try and we methodically tried each and every one with absolutely no change in his plucking behaviour. He continues to pluck, let the feathers grow in and then pluck them out again. For about two years he has neither gotten better nor worse and seems to remain the same. It is possible that the problem has been fixed but the plucking has now become a bad habit but we'll never know for sure.

To take Pickles to the vet is an all day trip to get there, and an all-day trip to return. I have relatives to stay with but the trip - including gas, expenses and vet bill - cost over one thousand dollars. Pickles was great all the way there and all the way back. He was stuck in his travel cage next to me for many hours at a time and never seemed to mind – unless I looked directly at him. If I looked at him, he would do that annoying squawk so any time I had to check on him, I had to look at him through the corner of my eye. I was told that he was very good while staying at the vet's office for those three days and that he spoke a bit but was mostly content to sit and watch all the action going on around him.

Will we ever figure it out? I don't know, but we keep trying.

*Mom stubbed her toe on a chair and fell to the floor, writhing in pain. As she lay there, I got very concerned so I got down from my cage, walked over to her and looked her deep in the eyes and told her, "It's okay mom. You need to let go. We'll all be fine without you – it's time to let go now".*

<u>Dead Give-Aways</u>

As Pickles' fans know, Pickles is never caged except when he asks for it at night to go to bed. Because of this, incidents happen now and then when he climbs down to the floor in search of something or somebody. He almost always gets caught right away for several reasons. When he suddenly gets quiet, I check on him. If I hear him saying, "Get back up!" or "Stop it!" he's busted. The flapping sound of wings or the clicking sounds of his nails on the floor area are always a sure sign that a bird's on the loose and, when all else fails, Neeka Dog will always bark to rat him out. But, he continues to do it now and then and I would discourage him a little more if it were so darn cute and entertaining *most* times.

Pickles got me one time. I had taken a shower and forgot to close the screen door between the livingroom (his home base) and the kitchen so when I got out of the shower and heard his happy little 'chew' sound that sounded like it was coming from the diningroom, I figured I'd better go check it out. Pickles loves a good game of hide-and-go-seek and the diningroom is perfect for that because today I had been packing stuff up for storage and there were boxes and lots of junk to make good hiding spots.

I just stood back for a little while, waiting for him to snicker or nose laugh because he gets so excited when he thinks I can't see him but when I couldn't hear him, I went searching for him. I couldn't find him anywhere and eventually, I walked into the livingroom and happened to glance up and spot him on top of his cage. He had fooled me by throwing his voice again.

He tried to fool Neil one day. Pickles was playing with his plastic whiffle-like ball with bell inside. He was shaking it around like a maraca and playing beautiful music in his ear but eventually got bored and dropped it so

Neil picked it up and put it in Pickles' talon bucket inside the cage so that Neeka Dog wouldn't get it.

A little while later Pickles had a plan and Neil watched it unfold. Pickles was cocking his head and staring at the floor and thinking about getting down. He climbed into his cage, walked across a perch to his bucket, picked up the ball in his beak and then threw it to the bottom of the cage. Then he climbed down the bars to the bottom of the cage door opening and nonchalantly reached his talon over, picked up the ball, pretended to play with it for a half a second, threw it to the ground and said, "oops!" and then made out like he had to retrieve it but all the while, it was just a ruse to get to the floor to investigate other stuff. He climbed down about 6 inches before Neil yelled at him to get back up. Dumb bird. He just HAD to choose the noisy bell, couldn't have used the foam one – noooooooo. Busted again.

If we are with Pickles when he's sitting on the back of the couch, he will try to chew on the curtains but if he flies over there without anyone noticing – I usually notice but let him think he's getting away with it – he will sit there for an hour and never even *look* at the drapes. That tells me that it's only fun for him if we are there to watch him and get all uptight about it.

He loves the back of the couch because he can look outside, talk to wild birds and yell and bark at anybody walking down the street so it was a little upsetting when I changed the furniture around and placed the couch against a different wall. Even though he had seen me move it, I guess he figured that if he flew over to the big window, the couch would suddenly materialize for him to land on. But it didn't. He hovered in one spot as long as he could, until he ran out of gas, crashed and burned and had to do the walk of shame back to his cage.

He refused to give up. Every day he would fly to it and every day it still wasn't there and every day he'd get stuck hanging on the window frame and every day he needed my help and every day I just left him there and laughed at him and every day it took him a few minutes to realize he could just let go and his wings would carry him back to his cage and every day, I'm sure he cursed the day I was born.

Pickles really took advantage of the time I threw my back out. It became obvious to him that if I was lying on the couch, chances were that I couldn't move off it – not without help. He would get that look in his eyes and I would tell him, "Don't you dare, Pickles." He'd get a sneaky look on his face and his eyes would go all hooded or squinty and he'd start to climb down the bars, head first, stopping every few seconds to tease me and I would yell at him to, "Get back up!" But he'd ignore me and once on the ground, he would take exaggerated long, slow steps toward the kitchen, glancing over his shoulder just daring me to stop him. Once in the kitchen, I couldn't see him anymore except when his head would slowly look around a wall to mock me.

He tried it one too many times though because one day he thought I was on the couch paralyzed and when he climbed down and headed for the kitchen, he glanced back over his shoulder to taunt me and there I was, closing in on him. He freaked, screamed like a little girl and leapt straight up and into my hands before he knew what happened.

I was playing with Neeka on the bed in the bedroom and I guess Pickles decided he wanted to join us because I heard his nails clipping along the floor. But then it stopped. A couple of minutes silence and I figured I'd better go investigate. I arrived in the kitchen to find him standing with his head in the gap between the fridge and the counter. Just standing there, not moving, sitting on his haunches, head in the dark. Ha! Heading to find us but gets sidetracked by a dark cranny.

*I was on my ropes in the diningroom and dad went to pick me up to go home and I bit him. I was having a good time where I was and didn't want to leave so I don't know why he was so surprised, especially considering my documented propensity to snap when aggravated. You're kinda big to go crying to mama, aren't ya?*

### Dirty Toes

Pickles calls Neil's Doritos, 'dirty toes'. He always wants one but Neil hardly ever gives him any because we don't like him eating junk food. He knows the things on the end of our feet are also 'toes' and we also have a game where we try to grab his little 'chicken toes'.

One evening, Pickles was intent on climbing down his cage to the floor. He had been sitting above, cocking his head and mumbling something about dirty toes. Curious as to what he was up to, we pretended not to notice him climbing down and walking across the floor behind his cage. He walked right up to the end piece of a banana that he had tossed earlier, put his beak up to it, announced, "Be right back, dirty toes!" turned and headed back up his cage.

I have no idea why he would have called the piece of banana 'dirty toes' except that being the end piece, it kind of looked like a toe. It was funny too, because it had started to go brown so it now looked like a 'dirty' toe.

After climbing back up on his cage, I guess he figured he got away with something and decided to climb back down again. We were watching TV and may not have noticed except that he blew it by announcing to the toy he'd been playing with, "Be right back!" as he started his descent, head first down the outside cage bars. We immediately told him to, "Get back up" and he echoed, but much louder, "GET BACK UP!" and then obeyed himself.

*I kept asking for some of mom's rice crackers and then I'd just toss them and ask for more then the last time she handed me some, I bit her finger when she handed it to me. She refused to give me any more and told me I was a nasty bird. Whoa, whoa, WHOA! Like where did THAT come from??*

## Fun In The Aviary

Once the nice weather rolls around and it's warm enough for Pickles to go outside in his aviary, he will nag at me non-stop to go outside. He had been in his aviary a couple of times this spring and then suddenly the weather turned cold and rainy so he had to stay indoors for a few days. He doesn't understand, of course, he just thinks I'm being mean so I have to endure his abuse until the weather changes. The first nice day, I took him outside and the first thing he did, as a couple of young girls in skimpy t-shirts walked by, was his pogo stick sound (doing, doing, doing) to the beat of their bouncing boobs. Who's going to believe it's a hidden parrot? So, why bother explaining.

The sun is high and there's no shade for me to sit in near the aviary so I went and sat on a bench situated across the pond and back in the trees. Pickles sat quietly preening and I sat quietly watching. A crow landed on the clear Plexiglas aviary roof, right above Pickles, and cawed to his friend who had landed on the fence nearby. The moment the crow cawed, Pickles immediately cawed back from his camouflage below, startling the crow into tangling his feet and doing a face plant while trying to sidestep on the slippery surface to look at Pickles below. I burst out laughing because it was just so comical - I mean, how does a bird with wings and the ability to lift off, end up in a face plant? – but when I laughed, it scared the crow off.

A little while later, I was throwing the trout some pellets when some guy stopped and called over the fence,

"I got your books from the library in town and read about your parrot" he said.

"Cool" I answered.

"Is he in the aviary?" he asked.

"Yup, sitting top corner" I informed him.

"Oh yeah, I see him!" he exclaimed.

"Yup" I said.

"I read about how silly he gets outside and how he embarrasses you all the time" he said with a chuckle.

"Yup, he can be quite the little devil" I chuckled back.

"Has he been talking today?" he asked, eagerly.

"Oh yeah" I said, looking at Pickles and waiting for him to get started.

Silence.

We both stare at Pickles.

"Do you think he'll talk again?" he asked, hopefully.

"I'm sure," I answered.

Silence. Uncomfortable silence.

"He doesn't look much like a parrot, does he?" he remarked as he turned and walked away.

I walked over to the aviary and said, "Did you hear that Pickles? He said you don't look like a parrot." "Caw" he replied.

*I know it's hard to understand dad but yes, I like my wooden house that's attached to the wall where I can approach it from my ropes and boings in the diningroom. When I see it from that side, it is perfectly safe. But when you try to put me in it from the opposite side, it is a monster that wants to eat me. Can't you SEE that????*

## A Fun Ride

We find that rather than try to clean cages in the house, it's easier to just roll them outside to clean and hose down, especially since we put laminate floors in and they aren't supposed to get too wet. Toys and all can be cleaned and then left to dry in the sun and it's easier to clean the floors and walls where the cage sits without working around it.

The last time Neil took it outside to clean, I guess he must have loosened the top perch somehow (which only screws in on one side) because just as Pickles climbed in to go to bed, the perch crashed to the ground with Pickles riding it all the way, wide-eyed and hanging on for dear life! I'm sure his life must have passed before his eyes and no doubt he was regretting not even getting started on his bucket list but once he hit the ground he only sat there, stunned, for a few moments. When he regained his senses, he grabbed the end of his perch and tried to drag it up the cage bars in an attempt to either repeat this fun ride, or merely to have his favorite roosting perch back where it belonged.

*When mom bent over to pick the toys up from the bottom of my cage, I ran like a spider down the outside cage bars and bonked her hard in the head with my beak which made her straighten up fast and bang her head on the*

70

*top of the cage door opening which caused her to roar her anger and throw my maraca against the wall and crack it. Just a word of warning to those birdies who are stuck in the house with their mommies during a heavy snow – just cuz you're bored, it's best not to poke the bear.*

## Hot Pepper Kisses

Pickles isn't all that crazy about peppers of any kind but now and then he will eat them. What he really likes though is the seeds of any pepper so we always give him the pepper cores with the seeds attached. He's especially fond of hot pepper seeds and as everybody knows, this is the hottest part of the pepper.

One day, I had forgotten that I had given him a small, red, hot Birdy Pepper (yes, that is what they are actually called) and while we were playing on the couch, I gave him a nice kiss on the beak. Moments later, when my lips began to burn, I cried, "Owwww!" Pickles was on the back of the couch, at the same level as my head and he cocked his head, looked me in the eyes and said with contempt, "Oh, just stop it!" A sympathetic bird, he's not.

*Today I stared out the window, chased a ball, chewed stuff up, napped on the bed, ate some dry food, whined when mom&dad went out, cleaned my bum, got my nails clipped, ate my poop. Wait! I got mixed up. That's what my dog did all day.*

## He Who Must Be Obeyed

Neeka, our little six pound Min Pin, considers Pickles the Parrot the top dog around here. Neeka seemed to have picked up on this when he first came to stay 3 years ago when he was six weeks old. He obviously noticed how we run around, catering to Pickles – feeding him delicious food that isn't offered to dogs, handing him most excellent toys that he's not allowed to have and how we generally heeded to all Pickles commands and demands.

Pickles dictates bedtime, meal time and snack time. He tells us what lights to turn on or off, and when to do it. He is in charge of music and the stereo. We go outside to the aviary on his say so and wherever we are, we go home when Pickles decides we must do so.

Pickles calls the dog, reprimands the dog, feeds the dog and praises him. Neeka never looks to us for food while we're eating because we never give it to him but he knows that Pickles is much more generous so he sits patiently below, waiting for Pickles' offerings. Pickles also has the bestest toys and sometimes Neeka finds cool cast-offs on the floor. Neeka goes nuts playing with a large bead and Pickles enjoys watching so dismantling a toy for beads to toss is very rewarding.

Neeka probably knows Pickles' body language better than us and he definitely understands Pickles' sounds, both loud and subtle, better than we do. More and more, I notice Neeka reacting. Indeed, sometimes Neeka will react just by walking up to Pickles after hearing a small chirp or squeak and Pickles will acknowledge him in some small way, as if they have their very own way of communicating.

If Daddy goes out, Pickles always alerts us when he's arriving home. I know it when he says, "Daddy's home!" but Neeka knows it a split second before – from a small sound he makes or from his stance. Neeka can be with me in another room and the minute Neil starts to hand Pickles a snack, Neeka knows from the happy little 'choo' sound that emits from Pickles so he runs off, hoping for a dropped morsel.

When Pickles is ready to go to bed and tells us, "Lights off", Neeka immediately runs to the basket that the cage cover sits on because it's also where we discard Pickles' dirty toys so Neeka wants to inspect beneath the cover for anything new.

He knows the sound of Pickles' climbing down his cage or the sound of his toenails clicking on the floor and will awake from a sound sleep to alert me that Pickles is up to no good before I realize it myself.

If something is scaring Pickles – like a spider, or something outside the window, or whatever – Neeka can tell immediately and runs to see what dangers are lurking. Neeka has become a lazy guard dog and now relies on Pickles' alert to someone approaching the house before leaping to the window and taking on the role of protector.

Yes, Neeka is at Pickles' beck and call and if Pickles told him to jump off a bridge, his only obstacle would be the fence around the yard. Neeka is very obedient to Neil and I but if Pickles' offers a counter command, we're left in the lurch. Because, as far as Neeka is concerned, Pickles is Pack Leader Snack Feeder and He Who Must Be Obeyed.

*Mom made Flapper Pie and left it on the counter to cool. Flapper Pie! Now if ever there was a pie for birdies, it's Flapper Pie. The name says it all – it's GOTTA be mine! Well, I went for it and I figure it's called Flapper Pie cuz once you land in the middle of it, your wings get too sticky to fly and all you can do is flap – and splatter custard, graham crumbs and meringue over every square inch of the kitchen.*

### More Food Fun

Pickles is a bit of a fussy eater so food is always hit and miss with him. Baking birdie breads was always a great way of sneaking something like broccoli into his system, and I still make birdie breads, but mostly I rely on skewers these days. I place fruits and vegetables that he likes on the skewer but also foods he doesn't. He can't stand to leave anything undisturbed; everything must be chewed up and ripped off. He can't help but get some of the nutrients in his mouth, which means some amount of it is being absorbed but also, he will sometimes decide he likes a certain food after all because he has been getting used to the taste while shredding it off his skewer.

I always put peppers on it and he doesn't particularly like the peppers themselves but he loves the seeds. He will eat the seeds from any pepper – green, yellow or red bell peppers – and he especially likes hot peppers. We tend to forget when we've given him hot peppers and it's like he asks for kisses deliberately after he's eaten them, just to make our mouths burn. I wonder why it doesn't seem to affect them. I think it might, to some degree, because he tends to pin his eyes more and shake his head with the hot seeds.

He still refuses to eat broccoli for the most part. Sometimes, but ever so rarely, he will take a bite or two from the flower part. But mostly I buy it every week or two, we're not particularly fond of it so it ends up rotting, we throw it out and then we buy some more. I just can't seem to stop the dance.

If you've read my previous books, you know that we've always given Pickles snacks (pine nuts) for pooping on paper or pooping on demand when required. We would have him poop on a TV guide periodically; rather than have him poop on the couch while we had him down to play, or other such situations. We seldom reward him for pooping now as we felt he was getting too many pine nuts during the day and if we tried to hand him anything else for a reward, even if he liked it, he would throw it in our face.

The most annoying thing though, was that he would sit on the edge of his playstand, get our attention by telling us he was gonna "poop on the paper" then poop and ask for his snack. He would do this over and over and over until, in the end, he'd really have to get his booty shaking to get the teensiest little poop out, which would be smaller than the tiny pine nuts. It would have been okay if he *always* pooped on paper but if we weren't around, he pooped helter skelter, anywhere he pleased. Plus, we keep paper almost everywhere that he can poop on the floor so it's not like he deserves a reward for all the pooping going on.

We have tons of foraging toys that we have bought for Pickles over the years. Some are too easy for him and others drop the food to the ground after he has worked so hard to get at it. It seems that too many of them are like that. If the puzzle is particularly difficult, Pickles isn't interested in working that hard for food – even if I withhold certain treats for just this purpose. We bought him a foraging tray and screwed it into the side of his cage, on the outside. It has four different compartments, all of them opening in a different way, and it's fairly easy for him. The hard part is getting his beak inside to claim the pine nut reward but, for the most part, he prefers to use the tray as some fancy perch and will spend a lot of time perched on it after opening all the compartments. How this isn't painful for his little feet, with the slim edges, I don't know. If you were to ask him, he'd probably say he only does it to annoy me after I spend so much time, effort and money making or buying the perfect perches for him.

I think that bird spends most of his time conniving against me. He knows I won't let him have any of my coffee and he stopped trying to drink it many years ago except for recently when he decided he might like a drink after all and hopped over to my mug. I moved it away from him telling him that he can't have any because it is harmful to birds so he bit my hand, causing me to spill hot coffee in my lap. Probably his way of telling me that's it's not just harmful to birds.

He got even with me for being too lazy to cut up his banana bite size, just the way he likes it, and placing a big chunk of it on his cathouse instead. When I walked away, I didn't notice that he flung it to the kitchen floor so a couple of minutes later, as I walked across the floor with my bowl of Rice Crispies, I slipped in the banana sending my cereal flying through the air as I did the splits and waved my arms to keep my balance. I managed to stay on my feet but my milk and cereal plastered the kitchen and as I glanced at Pickles, he seemed to be thinking that the whole ordeal was both horrifying and real cool all at the same time, eventually deciding on real cool according to the happy head bobs.

76

I only give Pickles seeds once a week and eating them must be thirsty business because he goes back and forth from his seed bowl to his water bowl and because his beak is wet, all the seed husks glom on, making it look like he has warts or some other cool disease. But God help you if you serve him anything but cold seeds, straight out of the fridge. The last time I gave him room temperature seeds because I'd poured them into a bowl and got sidetracked, leaving them on the counter. I placed the bowl inside his cage and Pickles got all excited and scrambled inside to perch on the rim of the bowl. His head disappeared briefly but came back up with a squawk and then he stormed out of his cage to squawk again and glare at me in anger over my incompetence.

I took the bowl back out and refilled it with cold seeds out of the fridge and by the time I got back, he was hanging on the side of the cage door opening, waiting for me. I didn't dare stick my hand inside with the bowl because I had to get past him and I could tell that he was only waiting there to punish me with a bite. I had to stand there and wait it out but he wouldn't budge until I said, "Okay, forget it then" and pretended to walk away. He scooted back to the top of his cage and squawked once again while I quickly placed the bowl inside without losing any blood.

*Mom said that one of these days, when Neeka the Dog eats my poop, it's gonna make one of her friends so sick they'll blow chunks. I said – Cool! Anything I might like? Or does the dog get that too?*

Neeka, Wait!

77

Neeka is trained to wait until called when walking through doors or up and down stairs. This is so that he doesn't trip us up while bolting on stairs or through doors. Also, since he was a pup, to keep him from running down the driveway and out into the street, we reward him with a nice cookie once we're in the house. Now all he can think about, after jumping out of the car, is getting in the house as fast as possible to get that cookie. While returning home from an outing with Neeka, I walked through the door and in to the house and turned to release Neeka but he wasn't there. I walked back through the door and went looking for him then happened to glance back and see him standing inside the doorway. He had obviously slipped past me into the house before I could turn to release him but now he was sitting obediently inside the door rather than following me outside. I called him out then walked back in the house so he could wait this time and redeem himself. I turned to tell him, "okay' but he was gone again. I looked in to the livingroom and there he was, sniffing below Pickles' cage.

"Neeka! Get back here!" I commanded, and sent him back to the other side of the door where I told him to wait. He sat momentarily then shot back inside and straight over to Pickles cage again but this time I knew why. I tend to ignore sounds that come from Pickles, since there are always sounds coming from Pickles, but I had missed him doing the 2 short whistles we use to call the dog. Each time Neeka and I appeared at the door, Pickles called him over – obviously happier to see Neeka than he was to see me after being gone a few hours. And Neeka obviously wasn't fussy about who he obeyed as long as there was some sort of command and reward coming from someone.

*I don't know why but I was walking along the bottom of my playstand and I came across some of my poop. I stretched my head out, stuck my tongue out real far and very tentatively and gave it a little taste. Just then, I happened to notice mom looking at me with her face all scrunched up in disgust. Don't judge me, old woman. I've seen you eat liver.*

## Getting Parrots Back in Cage

Getting a bird to return to his cage seems to be a huge issue among parrot owners and every time I read or hear about someone at their wits end over this, I just shake my head and thank God that Pickles isn't like that. Then one day, I realized why he wasn't – and we'd just stumbled into it by accident.

Most people (including us, back in the beginning) enjoy their 'quality' time with their birds in the evenings, the time of day when they are most relaxed after a day at work or a day with the kids. Out comes the parrot and the fun interaction begins. He's been waiting all day long to get out of his cramped quarters and receive some interesting or loving attention so why the heck would he want to have it all come to a stop and go back in his cage?? He's certainly not tired and ready for bed because he's had all kinds of time to sleep and nap while stuck in the cage for the past 20 hours or more.

At the time of this writing, we've had Pickles just shy of ten years and he came to us at three months of age. Right from the beginning, he would come to work with us when we owned the fly shop. He had a cage there but mostly he perched or played on his playstand behind the counter but close enough to interact with people in the store. He had freedom, change of scenery, entertainment and company all day so by the time we got home from work, Pickles was no longer in need of much more attention because he was tired. Getting him in the cage and to bed was never usually a problem and if he decided he didn't want to go to bed, it didn't matter to us.

In later years, our career choices have been such that we tend to have a lot of time together or work in such a way that Pickles almost always has someone home with him. And because he is out of his cage the moment we are up in the morning and just hangs around the cage and playstand, we don't even put him in the cage when we go out. He is contained inside the livingroom, and separated from our little Min Pin dog, by a screen door we attached in the doorway. He has no desire to go wandering or chewing things – as a rule, he's uncomfortable away from his area when left alone – so he just sits or plays or stares out the window. So again, Pickles is out of his cage all day and perfectly happy to go to bed at night and in fact, tells us when it's bedtime and goes in on his own when he's ready.

The last couple of years, Pickles usually wants to go to bed immediately after having his supper, and suppertime is at 5:00pm. It doesn't matter what time of the year it is or what time the sun sets, bedtime is bedtime and it doesn't matter once he is covered. He likes going in and he may go straight to sleep or play or talk to himself or a combination throughout the evening but he is happy in there and he obviously enjoys his privacy. He's already spent all day with one or both of us so he doesn't feel the need to stay up any longer. As a matter of fact, and it's kind of insulting, we can go out all day and get home around dinner time and Pickles just yells for supper and demands his lights off and cage covered right after eating. He was out all day long and even though he didn't have company, he was tired of being out.

Now, we're pretty fortunate in those regards and it's been easier for us than most. Some people have bird rooms or aviaries and of course that can solve the problem but then, that can make it easier to ignore your bird when you feel like you're just too busy to 'deal' with them so it's easy and convenient to just avoid them. And by no means am I saying that anyone who has a separate bird room neglects their birds, I can just see ourselves tending toward leaving Pickles on his own a little more just because it might be more convenient at the time. It's like having a grandmother offer to babysit any time you want to get away, it's like hell,ya! We want Pickles interacting with us all day long and that is why he has ropes, boings or stands in most rooms and while it's not always a picnic around him, it's the way it is and the way we want it.

Now we did have the problem of getting Pickles into his cage for a brief time a few years ago - and I've written about it in my books - but to make a long story short, it all boiled down to allowing him to make his own decisions about being in or out of the cage and giving him his freedom. Once that was determined, we never had a problem with it again.

It seems to be a Catch22 situation for many people; they don't let their birds out because they can't get them back in the cage, and they can't get their birds back in because they don't let them out enough. Unfortunately, if this is the case, it is doubtful that this problem will ever be solved. If we deprive 'pet' birds of their freedoms, how can we contain them in small quarters to boot? All the toys and enrichment in the world, inside their cages, won't ever make up for human contact and freedom from the cage. Anybody who doesn't give a bird the appropriate amount of freedom shouldn't have a bird.

81

No matter what the excuse or reason. If someone has an excuse, then that excuse is the reason why they shouldn't have a bird. And getting more birds just so the first bird will have company and companionship is not good enough. When you bring a bird into your life, you have the responsibility to actually give him a life with you. You could kidnap someone and keep them in the lap of luxury but they could never be happy without their freedom – birds are no different.

*Mom got mad at me for telling her friend that she was ugly. You know mom, if you don't say it, I can't repeat it.*

## Peas

People always ask if we really have conversations with Pickles and I say yes, but sometimes it's like talking to someone who is mentally challenged. For instance, Pickles only gets peas every other morning for his breakfast but one day he got it in his head that he wanted some afternoon peas and kept saying, "Want some peas." I ignored him and gave him other things to eat but he kept telling me he wanted peas. I finally told him, "You can have some peas in the morning." He thought about this for a few seconds then piped up with, "Good morning!" I told him that saying it doesn't make it morning.

I don't think he believed me because in his mind he knows he only says 'good morning' in the mornings and never during the rest of the day so therefore, saying it makes it so. The rest of the afternoon he rambled on with, "Good morning! Want peas. Good morning! Want some breakfast peas."

At suppertime, I tossed some peas in with his meal. He went to his bowl and just stood there staring instead of digging in as he usually does. Finally he stuck his head in the bowl, came up with a pea, walked across his perch and dropped it in the water, walked back, grabbed another pea and hiked back to drop it in the water again. He did this until they were all gone which is unusual for him as he very seldom drops food in his water dish on purpose.

After he finished eating his dinner he walked over to his water bowl and said, "Fresh water peas" and walked away. Was he stating that there were peas in his fresh water, or had he been offering fresh water for the peas to drink? Who knows? Conversations with him can sometimes hurt your head.

*A really fun thing to do is hang on a toy and start flapping and screaming as if you're stuck and in a lot of pain. Then mom comes in and gets all upset and starts crying and everything cuz she can't get near you to see what's wrong. After awhile you sit up and start nose laughing and you feel real good cuz it was a really good trick.*

## The Craft Sale

A craft sale was hosted by the Senior's Centre in our small town of Logan Lake, BC so I decided to splurge the $5.00 it took to get a table for a book signing and packed up my husband (Neil) and Pickles. Pickles because he's the star of the books – indeed, he actually wrote the last one 'himself'- and Neil to officiate any trouble Pickles got into, keep him away from the books if I was busy, or to take him home if he got bored and cranky.

We walked through the aisle of vendors, to oo's and aw's, and down to our table at the far end to set up. Neil set the playstand on top of the table and placed Pickles on the top branch about a foot above our heads and in front of us, as I stacked books. Pickles readily stepped up onto the perch and surveyed the land in his regal, aloof manner while the masses surrounded him. Immediately, the questions started. Does he talk? Does he bite? Does he poop a lot? Does he fly? And, my personal favorite – Is that a pigeon?

I had just finished explaining how Pickles can fly but he seldom does (unless startled) when Pickles rose up in a flurry and gunned it down the length of the aisles, landed perfectly on a curtain rod, turned and waited with one foot in the air for me to come and rescue him. Always the way – tell someone Pickles does or doesn't do something and he exposes you as a liar. But what was really crazy was that not one person ducked or freaked out as he jetted by and two people actually put their hands up, offering him a landing strip. I mean, what's with THAT? With the obstacle course of people, I had been afraid of some startled or terrified backhands along the way.

By the time I got Pickles back to the table, customers started rolling in the door. Some people came specifically to buy a book so they knew about Pickles but others, those unsuspecting suckers, hadn't expected to see a parrot sitting amongst branches and if they didn't notice him as they walked by, Pickles made sure they did. His talking just blended in with the rest of the crowd noise so to get someone's attention, he had to resort to wolf whistles, loud phones, squawks, any weird noise he could come up - and of course, the fart. The room came to a standstill at one point when Pickles let out a loud alarm - the kind that's sends people scrambling, hands over ears, to find the off switch.

Once people noticed him, most wanted to visit with him. Some were good and just stood talking or listening, others stuck tasty little wiggly worm fingers in his face and others thought I was selling birds. Regardless, being the tallest in the room atop his high branch, he was pleased with all his minions below.

One kid cried out in dismay as Pickles turned his back to him and let go a boom-boom, "Ewwwww!" he shouted while Pickles shot back, over his shoulder, "Oh, just stop it". I think that's the hardest part for non-bird people, the constant pooping going on. And, it's not pretty.

All in all, Pickles was great. He beaked book pages as his own signature and behaved – as far as a talking parrot can behave. He stayed away from the books, he didn't fly again and he didn't demand to go home at any time. Neil took him for a walk-a-bout on his shoulder and Pickles enjoyed that but when they got to a perfume stand, Pickles insisted he wanted some of the 'juice' and got a little put-out that he wasn't offered any. At one point, while everyone was packing up and leaving and his audience was slowly disappearing, there happened to be complete silence for a moment which prompted Pickles to shout at the top of his lungs "Anybirdy home?!"

As I set him on his playstand when we got home, Pickles remarked, "Good, eh?" I asked him, "What's good, Pickles?" and he said, "Good party". Indeed it was.

*I think the universe exists for me. Don't get me wrong – you're all important too, but only as long as I am with you or talking to you. I don't know what everybody's doing when they're not around me but it really doesn't matter. It only matters what I'm doing and what I'm thinking. You guys are just 'extras' in my movie of life and I am the star. Take mom for instance – if I can't see her or hear her, she just goes into sleep mode until I need her for something.*

## Poor Daddy

Neil is probably the most patient man I know, especially when it comes to Pickles. He cares deeply for Pickles and will do anything to make him happy. Pickles adores his daddy and knows he's just a big softie. They didn't always have such a great relationship. It was great when Pickles was young but then Neil was going out of town to work for a couple of years and was seldom home. Pickles began to resent the time I spent with Neil when he came home for a weekend and took it out on him by biting him at every opportunity. Neil became fearful of him and even though he tried hard to get Pickles to like him again, he took many a bad, bloody and painful bite. It took some work, as I have described in my previous books, but we got things back to normal and they have been enjoying a great relationship for years now. But this *IS* Pickles we're talking about and even though he can be fun, and fun loving, he has his moments and we still suffer the odd bite now and then but Neil just goes with the flow.

He stubbed his toe one day and dropped to the floor in pain. As he lay there, face down, Pickles took this opportunity to climb down from his cage and jump on Daddy's back. Daddy didn't move and I guess Pickles was afraid he was dead or something and decided to find out by biting his ear. Daddy jumped up, screaming, and scared the heck out of Pickles who flew back up to the top of his cage and looked back at him, wondering what the big deal was.

Pickles loves to lie in bed with Neil. Sometimes he just lies on his belly and enjoys nice scratches, other times he likes to get under the covers and take a nice little nap and he also likes to play 'fort' where Neil makes a nice open tent for him to play or hang around in. Neil was under the covers and Pickles wanted to play 'fort' so the blankets were held up for him while he ran back and forth, climbed blanket walls and hung like a bat. After awhile it got hard on Neil's arm, holding the blanket up, and while Pickles was down around Neil's knees, Neil decided to drop the blanket and see if Pickles would find his way back in the dark. Neil laughed when Pickles headed the wrong way, down toward his feet but Pickles knew what he was doing. He knew he didn't need to know his way out, he just needed to bite Dad's toes and one little chomp raised the blanket and showed the way to freedom.

Neil did a really stupid thing one day. We both know that Pickles hates it when we're talking on the phone when it's *his* time and he's sitting with us. He can get very assertive about this, to the point of violence. Also, he will sit on your knee while you're on the computer and he'll be okay as long as you keep talking to him and paying him attention but of you stare at the computer screen, instead of him, for more than 30 seconds, he'll bite to get your attention back. I don't think Neil realized how Pickles was with the computer but he knew about the phone.

Neil was walking around with Pickles when he heard the email tone on his computer, indicating that he had a new message. He sat down to read it, resting his hand with Pickles on it, on his knee. The message required a quick phone call so Neil reached for his cel, dialed and then just as he put it to his ear, Pickles stapled himself to Neil's thumb, just below the fingernail. I heard the commotion from my office but didn't really think too much of it. I heard Neil going, "ow, ow, ow, owwwww" but I didn't know he had Pickles, that he was being bit by Pickles or how much pain he was in so I continued with my work. Eventually Neil showed up in my doorway, thumb in hand, wrapped in a towel with a look of excruciating pain on his face. I got up and followed him out to the kitchen while he explained what happened.

Once Pickles had bit down on Neil's thumb, he wasn't about to let go. Neil couldn't get him off and Pickles was grinding his bottom mandible and going for the bone marrow. When he finally got Pickles unattached, there was blood everywhere … his thumb, his pants, his shirt, the chair, the floor, Pickles' feathers and especially Pickles's beak. After Neil ran his thumb under water and got the blood to slow down enough to look, he realized that he should probably have stitches but it was Friday night and the nearest place to go was Kamloops, 45 highway minutes away, and he didn't want to spend his Friday night in a busy hospital. We ended up just taping it up and even though it oozed for a day or two, it ended up healing fine enough.

I'm sure Pickles figured a good time was had by all and I'm sure Dad learned his lesson but what Pickles learned was that you don't need to weigh more than 500 grams to bring a 200-pound man to his knees.

*Mom took me to a class presentation at a school in Kamloops yesterday and I visited with about 25 aspiring writers. At one point, I flew 3 laps around the room. It wasn't til I landed on mom's hand that I realized I had passed up about 25 opportunities to poop on heads.*

## Hiding in Plain Sight

There are so many toys, ropes, boings and things hanging on top of Pickles cage, on his playstands or hanging from the ceiling in the diningroom that sometimes it's difficult to find Pickles. I feel like such an idiot when I walk over to give him a snack and stand there searching every square inch for him just to finally find him right in plain sight, six inches from my face. I came nose to nose with him one time while leaning into his ropes to look for him. One of these days I'm gonna pay for that, considering his penchant for head bopping.

One time, he was playing on his diningroom ropes while I was making the bed and knocked something off the dresser. It made a loud bang when it fell to the floor and I knew it had startled Pickles because I heard wing flapping. I went to investigate and stood peering into his ropes searching for him until I heard a nose laugh behind me and turned to find him sitting on the little table that holds our mail. As usual, he was head bobbing in delight because I couldn't find him and this is the most amusing thing in the world to him.

*Mom thinks she's so smart but she doesn't seem to understand the difference between 'distraction' and 'positive reinforcement'. I was sitting on the bottom of my cage doorframe and kept grabbing the newspaper and ripping it up and spilling guck on the floor. She would go get me a snack and put it in my bowl to distract me and get me to climb up off the bottom of the cage. I got a nutriberry, turnip fry, roasted carrot and roasted potato before she realized that I kept returning to the scene of the crime in hopes of being*

89

*offered another reward. It was fun while it lasted and until she wised up but now I must find a new ruse.*

### Ropes and Closets

I have so many fancy toys for Pickles, thousands of dollars worth, but he plays less and less with them as he gets older. I still try, I still buy him things that I think he might like and I still make toys for him all the time too. He barely looks at store bought toys, especially toys made of hard plastic, acrylic or hard wood. Sometimes he'll take a liking to the toys I make and they're usually made of cotton rope, sisal, soft and chewable wood and some easily chewed plastic and beads. But I wouldn't call that playing; it's more like chewing.

There's one toy he loves to play and fight with but I won't give them to him anymore because he always gets hurt. I think everybody's seen those dice hanging off chains, hanging off an umbrella of acrylic. They look very much like those mobiles you hang above a baby's crib and they turn gently to music or just sway ever so slightly in a light breeze, something to contemplate and calm. But not the ones for birds. You don't just sit and gaze at them; you attack them viciously, sending all 5 dice violently in all directions at the same time as you scream bloody murder. You lunge at them, striking like a cobra but no matter how fast you are at pulling your head back, there's another dice already orbiting at warp speed, right into the side of your head. This makes you angry. Before this, you were just being polite but now you're out for blood and revenge. You strike furiously at anything swinging your general direction, usually missing and getting sucker punched from behind.

Sometimes you can manage to get them all going around evenly, like pushing along a tetherball once you have it racing on it's orbit above your opponents head – all you do is just slightly beak it as it goes by, just enough to keep it in motion but you're seldom that lucky. No. You're just all wings and beak and dice and it's all fun and games until someone cracks a beak. Yeah, I had to stop letting Pickles play with those. Besides, it's hard explaining the black eyes. I may as well tell people that he walked into the corner of a cupboard. I see the way they look at me; I feel the shame. And it's not like you can hang cotton balls on rope or something soft enough not to hurt when it hits but they're too light, basically moving in slow motion.

He still likes his stainless steel bucket of toys, which is attached to the bars near his favorite roosting spot under covers at night. But again, he's not really playing; he's chewing on stuff. The only thing he 'plays' with is his little plastic maraca.

So, toys aren't as important to him as they once were and he prefers hanging around, and hanging off, ropes and boings – especially if they have bells attached to them. Most of the time he just sits nicely and talks to us or preens or naps but now and then he gets pretty animated. He'll hang off something and then flap his wings to get it swinging in circles or back and forth and it he hits something now and then, that's okay by him because that's really what he's trying to do anyway. And if he's swinging on a rope, trying to reach that painting when Dad happens to walk around the corner just in time to take it in the solar plexus, well … BOOYAH! Extra bonus.

Swinging and screaming is great fun, especially if I'm out of the room, because it's causes a huge reaction from me and he knows it. The minute I come running to see why he's hurt, he sits up straight, head bob laughing. Seriously. He may as well be throwing his head back, holding his gut with tears streaming down his face because he seriously thinks this is hilarious.

So sure, we seem to take the brunt of his antics a lot of the time but he can also be his own worst enemy. Like the time he sat smugly atop one of his big bells, chewing on the rope it hung from while I warned him, several times, to stop. I swear it was like watching a cartoon where the character hangs mid-air with huge, shocked eyes in the split second before the final thread breaks. Down he went in a crumpled heap of feathers, too scared to let go of the bell as if it will do his flying for him. He always fluffs up as you go to fetch him, the fluffing to indicate how he meant to do that and what fun it turned out to be but his eyes tell the story of total shock that he even survived his own stupidity.

But Karma was at its best the time Pickles was hanging totally still and I walked right into his ambush. I was walking around the ropes to get to another room but I flew too close to the sun. I almost lost an ear that day. I screamed so hard and my hand flew up in reflex so suddenly that Pickles was half smacked and half torn in two from pulling my head away from him, and scared half to death by my screaming. Or, perhaps I should say, scared the poop out of him because as I glanced back at him, bloody ear in hand, he pooped. An upside down poop. An upside down poop that hit him smack in the beak. I've never seen such a thing, didn't even know that such a thing could happen but there was my parrot with poop streaked across his chin, cheek and beak. I actually laughed through my pain and didn't even care when he sat up and managed to shake some of it on me. I felt really bad that I had kind of smacked him when I reacted without thinking, but not bad enough to clean him up before I cleaned myself.

Like I said though, whether he plays with them or not, I have boxes and boxes of toys for him and I'm always changing them around, taking some away and trading for different ones. I had taken a few talon toys off the bottom of his cage and I had him on my hand when I went to get some clean ones to throw in his bucket. I keep all his talon toys in a very large hope chest and when I opened the lid, Pickles almost fell off my hand in excitement. As a matter of fact, I couldn't get him to sit upright on my hand; he kept throwing himself upside down in an attempt to get closer to the colorful treasure. I tried to grab a couple of items and hightail it out of there but Pickles wouldn't have it and I got a little nip in the finger as an order to drop him inside. I didn't want an angry, nippy, upside down bird on my hands so I quickly placed him inside to save myself.

Then, of course, there was no getting him out of there. He ran around, or at least tried to run around as it was sort of like running on top of all the balls in the ball pit at McDonald's so he kept sort of falling in amongst things but he'd pull himself up and head to the next items. All that stuff wasn't enough though, in his haste to see what lay below, he started to toss everything he could out of the hope chest. I sat on the edge and let him play for awhile but there's no way he wanted to stop investigating so I tried to get him to step up to leave. No amount of cajoling was going to get him out of there so I closed the lid and sat on top, hoping he'd whine to get out. All I heard was a quick shuffle then dead silence. After a couple of minutes I thought, "Heyyyyyy, I know that shuffle sound – that's the feather fluffing he does to take a nap!" I opened the lid to find him lying like a chicken in a nest, all fluffed up and half asleep. Man, how he loves his closed closets, cupboards and chests. It's like, dark is the coolest toy EVER!

I've basically banned Pickles from the hall closet now. He just can't help but chew on the towels and sheets I keep in there and when I put some old towels on top of the good stuff so he'd chew that instead, it's like he knew I was up to tricks so he started removing the door frame splinter by splinter instead. Close the door on him and he's in seventh heaven but I can't just let him sit in the dark for hours so I seldom let him in there anymore, even when he almost breaks his neck grabbing for the door or door knob anytime I walk by with him on my hand. There was one exception.

I had been cleaning house and finally threw myself on the couch and lay there, face down. After a few minutes, Pickles got tired of being ignored because he loves cleaning day and helps out best he can by chatting and giving you direction so he flew off his cage and went for the moon landing. (He's done this before and, as a matter of fact, takes advantage of this position every chance he gets.) There he stayed, refusing to move from my butt but moving just out of reach of my hands. I couldn't roll over without squishing him and I couldn't reach him so all I could do was stand up. That didn't really get me anywhere because I still couldn't reach him to get him off my butt where he was hanging, head down and butt up. So now I couldn't sit and all I could do is walk around with a parrot stuck to my butt. Only one thing to do; I opened the linen closet, stuck my butt inside and Pickles immediately jumped on to a shelf. With a heavy sigh, I went and got a kitchen chair to sit on outside the closet. From there, I could supervise Pickles and argue with him about what he could and could not do while he was in there. I'm not sure what's worse, a butt bird or a closet bird.

Ropes and closets. Who needs bird toys when you've got ropes and closets? I have a walk-in closet in the bedroom but Pickles likes to run real fast into it.

*Jeez, Pickles, we finally find a nice, family restaurant that allows you to dine with us and you insult the waiters and the food and then you throw food all over the place – why don't you like it there?  Because, Mom – they treat me like family.*

## Scary Stuff

I don't know what it is with that bird. If it won't harm him, he's afraid of it – if it's bad for him, he just *has* to have it – in fact, he *needs* it and will surely die without it. He got angry at me when I got too close to him with my nail file and yet, the same day, Neil was painting in the livingroom and thought nothing of leaving a big, scary, bright yellow can of paint open behind him, confident that Pickles wouldn't be brave enough to go near it, and turned around to find Pickles perched on the rim, practically upside down in his attempt to check out the paint that was left at the bottom of the can.

He's afraid of the 4 litre (3 gallon) milk jug if you're holding it close to him while he's on the counter but if it's sitting on the floor with all the other bags of groceries you've just brought in, the plastic cap has to be chewed off and ruined so that the milk has to be poured into other containers to preserve it.

We make our own bread and do so with our big, clunky, loud bread maker. We've had it for almost two years and it just never happened that Pickles was near it when it was kneading loudly but one day, while he was on my hand, I went to check on the dough. I was worried that it would scare Pickles into taking flight so I held him away from the machine while I opened the lid. Pickles almost fell off my hand trying to reach close enough to inspect the moving dough inside. You've got to be kidding, I thought but I slowly brought him closer to get a good look. He immediately tried to jump inside the box but I held him away from it. He was upset at first but soon he was dancing to the beat of the beating dough.

I don't usually wear a towel on my head outside the bathroom. I wrap my hair in the towel while I dry myself off after a shower and get dressed, and then I take the towel off and comb my hair out before I leave the bathroom. One time, before I could remove my towel, Neil called me into the livingroom and when I walked in, Pickles freaked out, started flapping on top of his cage and ended up with lift-off right into the corner, leaving poop on the wall as he fluttered down to the floor. I literally scared the poop out of him.

I whipped the towel off, threw it on the couch, picked up Pickles and sat him on my lap to calm him down. He calmed down right away, once he saw the towel was no longer on my head, then immediately ran to jump on it where it laid next to us on the couch. You see, towels are for swinging on so he immediately grabbed a bunch in his talon and laid on his side waiting for me to pick up the towel and swing it in the air with him on it. Head towel – bad. Swinging towel – good.

*I have decided to stop throwing stuff, especially food, at the walls and on the floor. Said no parrot ... ever.*

## Sound Bites

Parrots pick up the craziest sounds. Sometimes Pickles will spend months picking up new sounds and show little interest in his words. He gets a lot of his material by just listening to things going on in the neighborhood, whether that be wild birds, barking/howling dogs, mechanical sounds and alarms, whistling, tires screeching or kids' playful squeals but most of his repertoire comes from TV, and mainly commercials.

I flipped when a new TV commercial started to air because it contained the sound of a dentist drill and I hate dentists so much that I had all my teeth pulled and then I was fitted for dentures at a young age – just to avoid drills and needles (not to mention that burning smell, the drool, gloved fingers in your mouth rubbing on saliva then smearing it across your face every time he changes positions, those cardboard x-ray films that they make you chomp down hard on and it's like chomping on a small knife blade. All those scary looking tools laid out on the tray right in front of you and while your dentist's out of the room, you're left to ponder what pain each one of them is capable of inflicting. I could go on about saliva suckers, those rubber wall thingies they string on your teeth, trying to spit in the sink with a frozen mouth, the dentist's bad breath in your face – let's face it, there is absolutely nothing pleasant about going to the dentist) but, I digress. So, once I heard the new commercial, I knew I was destined to listen to that sound over and over, possibly for the rest of my life. And so far, I haven't been wrong.

You never know what sounds are going to interest Pickles. I was half asleep, early in the morning and heard Neil watching a tennis match but when I mentioned it to him a little later, he told me there was no tennis on that morning. Pickles not only picked up the sounds of tennis but he picked up the sounds of the best grunters and screamers. For the next few weeks we not only had to listen to the squeaky runners on the tennis court but also had to relive, over and over, the previously broadcast match of Maria Sharapova and Victoria Azarenka playing each other at the Australian Open.

I once took bread out of the bread maker early enough to ruin the loaf – 2 series of 5 beeps is the signal to remove the bread so I did what I was supposed to do. It wasn't until I heard the same series of beeps about a half hour later that I realized I'd been duped.

Pickles has this weird way of walking when he's on the floor; a good part of the time is spent walking backwards and/or walking backwards in circles. A couple of steps forward then 5 or 6 backwards, a step or 2 forward, a do si do, an allemande left then circle your partner and eventually he gets to wherever he's going. We would stand above him laughing and doing the beep beeb sounds for a vehicle backing up so now and then he'll entertain us by walking backwards and announcing his intentions with the beep beeps himself. Then, all spring and summer this past year there have been crews working on the hillside practically across the street from us. I hate that we can't enjoy a nice quiet day outside - and it starts at 6:00am, before I'm awake – so by Friday evening, I'm breathing a sigh of relief and looking forward to the silence of nature for a couple of glorious days. But not to be. Pickles felt the need to carry on the work of these noble contractors so my weekend was spent listening to BEEP BEEP BEEP BEEP BRRRRRRR

BANG BANG BEEP BEEP BEEP BEEP.

I heard him making some sounds recently, which sound kind of like rapid gunfire. If he perfects that sound, I'm a little concerned about our next school presentation.

But all in all, we really enjoy all the sounds Pickles makes and he's seldom annoying. I have fallen asleep on the couch, many a time, while listening to Pickles. One of the cutest sounds he's made lately turned out to be quite the joke when one day he asked to go outside to the aviary and I told him, "No, because it's too hot". He knew immediately, from us making his supper, to start blowing on it to cool it down. I say it's too hot outside? No problem. Whffffff whffffff whffffff

*Whenever I get startled into flying off my cage or playstand, I fly for a bit and then usually land on the floor somewhere in the house. Once I've made my landing, I usually make noise so Mom or Dad can zero in on the sound and find me in case they don't realize I flew off. Sometimes I cluck like a chicken, sometimes I quack like a duck or bark like a little dog or maybe I'll caw like a crow – whatever suits my fancy at the time. Today I squeaked like Neeka Dog's squeaky toys and Dad just thought it was Neeka playing so he didn't come to find me so I had to walk all the way home ... backwards ... cuz I'm pretty sure monsters were trying to sneak up on me.*

## Stop

It's well known that Pickles hates getting wet. Sure, he'll go in his birdbath in the aviary but he only succeeds in getting his feet and beak wet. Same thing if he goes in the kitchen sink – he will run back and forth on his sink branch, in and out of the water dripping out of the tap, but he still only gets his feet and beak wet for the most part. That leaves the spray bottle, which he doesn't like, but it's the only way to get him wet.

I thought he was particularly clever one day when I was spraying him. He was quite indignant and he kept lunging for the bottle to make me stop so finally, I did. As soon as he realized he wasn't being sprayed anymore, he said, "Stop?" I said, "Yes" and he said, "Good!"

*Pickles' Facebook posts while Mom had a broken arm ...*

*Since Mom broke her arm, she figures if she can't play on the computer, nobody can play on the computer so she keeps them turned off. I snuck on though – cuz, with a broken arm, it takes forever for her to shower. She doesn't have a cast cuz the break is up near the shoulder so they only give her a sling for that. I was disappointed at first cuz I thought it might make a cool slide but then I decided a cool sling fort is even better. And, if I nip or tickle Mom while I'm in the fort, I can make her jump which causes her to make an awesome screaming sound. Dad says it's a scream of pain but I know a happy scream when I hear it. Because Mom only has 50% of her arms, I am able to have 50% more fun before she can stop me. Because of this, I was able to explore the cereal shelf and I discovered that I've become allergic to Cheerios because I felt sick after eating, like, 100 of them. I will*

100

*try to sneak back on the computer in a few days. Miss you guys.*

*I snuck back on the computer while Mom is drying and styling her hair – that will take awhile with a broken arm. Yesterday, Mom asked me if I wanted to go for a walk. Like, duh. I stepped up on her hand and we started in the diningroom, looking out the window at the wild baby butt birdies outside then the phone rang. Mom couldn't answer it cuz she can't use her broken arm and I was using the other one so she tried to get me to step down. No bloody way was I stepping down when I was promised a walk, dammit! So, while Mom was trying to get all fancy with tricks to get me to step down on my ropes with tasty snacks and songs and dancing, I just looked up at her with my sweet, dumb face while the answering machine cut in and took the message. It was Dad calling from Kamloops so Mom figured she would continue taking me for my walk around the house and call him back on his cel when we were through. We had a wonderful walk and I got to play in each room of the house so I was happy to go back to my cage and have a nice lunch of apple and oatmeal. I gots my lunch but Mom didn't get hers cuz Daddy had been calling to see if Mom wanted him to bring her Burger King and by the time Mom called him back, he was already on the highway heading home empty handed. Too bad, so sad, Mom. That'll learn ya not to break your arm again.*

*If your Mommy has a broken arm and she's eating a bowl of Jello on her lap and you fly over and land in her Jello and start eating it? There's not much your Mommy can do about it, except cry over spilt Jello.*

*Since Mom broke her arm, Dad has been feeding me in the mornings but this morning, Mom got up earlier and let me out of the cage. I waited and waited for my breakfast but she just sat on the couch, watching TV. Finally I said, "Somebody go get some breakfast!" She looked at me all surprised and stuff when I said it that way and I don't know why since I've always known all those words so it was just a matter of putting them together properly. She didn't make my breakfast but she got Dad up and he got busy in the kitchen. I got all excited when he walked in the room and I ran inside my cage to wait for my breakfast dish of peas but he walked right past me with coffee and toast for MOM. Next time I have to be more specific and demand that somebody go get ME some breakfast. After all, I AM the alpha around here.*

*Mom, I'm sorry I climbed inside your broken arm sling and then hung upside down on the outside of it and then chewed a hole in it and then bit you when you tried to remove me from this wonderful toy and I thought real hard about it and decided to forgive myself.*

*I was sitting on the back of the couch while Mom was eating her hot dog. I decided I wanted to try this delicious looking thing and I obviously wasn't being offered any. I figured this would be a good time to go for it as I may as well take advantage of Mom's broken arm and the fact that she has lost 50% of her defense so after a few moments of eyeing the situation and planning the assault, I dove for her shoulder and reached for the hotdog in one swift movement. I hadn't expected the wiener to slide so easily out of the bun, nor for it to be so hot so I flung it with a loud squawk. It flew into the air, landed on the coffee table where it slid across the surface leaving streaks of ketchup and mustard until it fell to the ground on the other side with a thump that attracted Neeka Dog who snapped it up and ran to his bed to eat it, leaving Mom holding an empty bun. It didn't work out anything like how I played it out in my mind – especially the part where the dog reaps the fruits of my labor.*

*Since Mom broke her arm, I not only don't get hardly any computer time these days but I don't get much attention from her either. And Dad's been outside a lot, working on the shed and decluttering stuff so I've been left to entertain myself more than usual lately. Mostly I sit on my ropes and boings and swing myself really hard in circles or back and forth. It's lots of fun but I guess I've been getting too carried away and I've ended up falling a few times. It's scary sometimes but after we all get over the initial shock and we all realize I'm okay, I realize how fun and hilarious I am. Except Mom doesn't find it all that hilarious when she has to pick me up and then I won't step down because I miss being with her as much as usual. I would step down for a good snack but Mom can't hold me and offer a snack with the other arm so she gets stuck with me until Dad rescues her. Sometimes I think she broke her arm just to make me miserable.*

### The Bathroom

Pickles doesn't really like the bathroom except for the counter and sink which we never allow him on because there's always too many interesting, but 'can't have', items scattered all over it and let's face it, the bathroom counter isn't the cleanest place for a bird. He's getting more and more blasé about 'Pickles in the Mirror' as time goes by and he only tolerates the shower rod while someone takes a shower – as long as the acid-like drops of water didn't splash and burn his delicate dirt encrusted skin and feathers. Heaven forbid.

So, he doesn't particularly care about going in the bathroom, unless the door is closed, somebody's in there and he hasn't been invited. Often, when one of us is in there, the other will take Pickles down the hall on their hand where Pickles can knock on the door. He really gets to banging his beak hard in-between hollering, "Hello? Zat you? Hello? Anybody?" and then he wants you to move your hand down low towards the floor then straight back up slowly, almost to the roof, while he makes a cool scraping sound by dragging the tip of his beak the whole way. Then more banging until someone inside cracks the door open enough for Pickles to stick his head and neck through, shake his tail in excitement as he exclaims in delight, "I seeeee youuuuu!" This kind of bathroom activity is acceptable to him.

However, he *loves* the counter, (after all, it *is* a counter and counters are THE best entertainment in the world – next to closets) and he gets so angry when you won't set him down on it. When we first got him, I let him play on the counter while I brushed my teeth but he was into everything, taking advantage of my occupied hands, which were holding a water glass and toothbrush. After that, he was never allowed back on it no matter how hard he tried or complained – until just recently.

In a moment of weakness, I allowed him on the counter while I brushed my teeth. It lasted until I bent over to spit and in a flash, Pickles had grabbed my toothbrush. He was in such a panic to rip it out of my hands that he totally forgot to hang onto it as he snatched it and the momentum of his head sent it sailing straight into the toilet – and he went after it! He Who Detests Water, actually flapped straight into the toilet water in his haste to retrieve what was forbidden.

Well, I don't know if he's just never noticed or recognized that there's water in there, or if he knew and then forgot, but the wide-eyed look of shock on his face made me smug enough to tell him, "Well, that'll learn ya!" as I scooped him out of the bowl.

I should have had the seat down as I usually do but I didn't, and it cost me a toothbrush – a really nice one and I have yet to find another one like it. Somebody is banned from the bathroom counter again.

*I was sitting on top of the kitchen counter door, half preening and half asleep while watching Mom make banana bread. She turned her back for a few seconds, just long enough for me to run across the counter, jump on the rim of the batter bowl and dig my beak into the batter. When she turned and saw me, she tried to get me to step up on her hand but I jumped over it and landed on my feet in the batter. "Well, look how ridiculous you look, Pickles – batter all over your beak, feet, half your belly and your wing tips" so I fluffed up and shook a bunch of it off, splattering some on Mom. NOW, who looks ridiculous?! Okay, still me. Regardless, I figure I had enough batter on me to rip her off for about ¼ of a piece of cake.*

### The Beak

If it wasn't for that beak of his, Pickles would be the perfect parrot. I'm convinced that, for the most part, Pickles doesn't really comprehend the strength of his own beak. Sometimes he can get very rough while playing and sometimes he'll bite to assert himself and I think he intends a little nip but it winds up a painful bite. He likes Neeka Dog and has no reason to hurt him but whenever he gets fairly close to Neeka, the neck stretches forward, beak open and tongue sticking out. I think it's his way of exploring, tasting, testing texture, smelling and feeling but he tends to lose control of his beak in the excitement. He always heads for Neeka's tail nub or his nose. He has never come close enough to touch Neeka but I would be afraid that Neeka would probably get hurt and I'm afraid Neeka would end up with one large nostril because that middle part between nostrils is just too soft and tempting for a beak.

After biting someone too hard, and getting a painful and angry reaction, Pickles always looks so surprised and confused. Sometimes he looks at you all indignant and as if thinking, *Don't be a baby. It's not as bad as getting hit in the head with an axe or something.* But other times, the look you get can be sheer hatred so you know he meant to bite you, and to exact the most pain possible. A grinding mandible clear to the bone is a dead give-away.

I got bit by mistake once when I approached him with a walnut while he was closely inspecting something in his empty food bowl and didn't notice until he turned to find my hand in his face. I guess he thought it was one of those flying, attacking monster walnuts because he took a chunk of my finger while defending himself. I was surprised because I didn't know it was possible to sneak up on Pickles (or any bird) and surprise them.

I was mortified after taking Pickles to the Vet because of the feather plucking he was doing to his chest. She prescribed a spray that we were to use on him - in a bottle that didn't spray far and worth about $50.00 so you needed to get up real close so that it wasn't wasted in the air or on the floor – and because Pickles hates getting sprayed, that meant dodging bites. THEN, the Vet tells us to sniff under his armpits to make sure the spray is working on his skin

106

bacteria. Now sure, there are times when Pickles can be really lovey and you can do things like this but you have to pick your times if you don't want to lose an eye.

Speaking of eyes – Pickles was sitting on my shoulder when I noticed a little scratch on his forehead but he wouldn't sit still long enough for me to take a good look at it. I got so involved and preoccupied with trying to see it and the next thing I knew, Pickles' beak was heading for my eye. It all happened in a split second and just as I was wondering how I'd look in an eye patch, Pickles licked my eyeball. I was incredibly relieved that I still had my eye and once I got over the initial shock, I had to chuckle because just thirty seconds earlier, I had told Pickles to sit still and look me in the eye. He must have thought I told him to 'lick' me in the eye.

Yes, we take our licks from him at times but every time we do, it's our own fault for not paying attention to his feelings, the situation and his body language.

*I know just the right whistle notes to hit to hurt little Neeka Dog's ears and make him howl and the more he howls, the louder I get until we're making the most beautiful music anybody ever heard but does Mom appreciate it, or sing along or dance to it? No. She says it hurts her ears too and she yells, "Cut it out – both of you!" Neeka always stops but sometimes I keep it up because you always hurt the ones you love.*

Dancing Fool

107

Pickles will dance to the strangest things. I guess parrots can find music in many things. He loves it when we play music on the stereo, he'll dance to some musical commercials, he has a few of his own music toys that he can press with his beak to make them play songs and sometimes, if there's a few hanging on top of his cage, he will run around pressing them all to get a real music racket going on.

I mentioned earlier that when I count the seconds out loud while his supper is warming in the microwave, he would dance to that. His Nana (my Mom) sent him a musical card with the song 'I Wanna Rock & Roll All Night, And Party Every Day' and he goes crazy dancing to that but I think the cutest thing is when we're driving in the car and I turn the on the windshield wipers or the turn indicators. I'm just the crazy lady in town who drives around on a nice sunny day with her wipers squeaking across the windshield, her left turn signal permanently blinking and a head-bobbing parrot in the passenger seat.

*I was playing on the kitchen counter while Mom and Dad were working in the kitchen and they gave me one of the oatmeal/pumpkin cookies Mom made for me. I ate most of it and then I ran around picking up the discarded pieces that were scattered all over the counter top and threw them, one by one, down to the dog. I like to watch the dog eat my orts. I dropped one crumb and it landed on the lid of the flip garbage can but Neeka Dog just sat there. I looked at him, then looked at the crumb, back at him, back at the crumb but as much as I tried to will him to go get it off the garbage lid, Neeka wouldn't go for it. This was upsetting to me and I spent a long time staring at them and trying to come up with a solution, all to no avail. How was I to know he's better trained than me?*

108

# The Hallway

Neil was sitting in a rocker in the living room, drinking his morning coffee when suddenly Pickles was startled by something and flew around the living room then headed down through the kitchen and down the hallway, landing on the floor at the very end of the hall. Neil figured that rather than get up and fetch him back, Pickles would eventually walk back on his own as he doesn't particularly like being alone on the floor.

From the rocker, Neil can see down to the end of the hall but it was early in the morning and still dark so he couldn't see Pickles, he could only hear the click, click of his toenails as he slowly made his way back. It takes a long time to go a short way because Pickles walks sideways, backwards and in backward circles when he's not quite sure if it's scary or not.

The clicking went on and on as Neil strained his eyes trying to get a glimpse of him until finally one eye started to shine through the black. Only one, because Pickles was walking sideways.

Neil continued to watch as the eye began to take on a ghostly body, just barely visible but slowly taking on a more solid form as he further emerged from the dark. I had gone to sleep in the bed in the computer room, as I often do when I am writing well into the night and just as Pickles passed my door, he heard me cough. He stopped dead, cocked his head to listen closer, walked back and stood staring at the door. He didn't move a muscle and stood staring for over fifteen minutes, waiting for any other sound that might emanate through the door.

Finally Neil walked down the hall to bring him back but Pickles wasn't budging. When Neil tried to get him to step up, he would just use the hand to jump up on and then spring over. Pickles was pretty sure I was in that room so he finally began knocking on the door with his beak.

Even though the door was open a crack, Pickles wasn't strong enough to push it open all the way but all the commotion had awakened Neeka (sleeping with me under the covers) who ran over and nudged the door open. Neeka suddenly appearing nose to nose with him out of nowhere, scared the heck out of Pickles and with a squawk and a flap, he was gone and definitely not waiting around to find out what fresh hell he had just narrowly escaped.

*Mom was eating a blueberry muffin and wouldn't give me any so I flew over and flung the whole muffin on the floor. If I don't get what's rightfully mine, I make sure nobody else gets it either.*

## What Are You Talking About?

Pickles definitely knows what he's saying a lot of the time but sometimes you wonder what's coherent and what's a fluke. Some days he barely talks, some days he never shuts up. Some days he speaks completely sensibly and other days he just babbles. But, there was one extraordinary day in which almost everything he said seemed to make sense even though I have to think that some of it was fluke. You be the judge.

It started at 5:00am in the morning when I turned on his UV light and lifted his cover to wake Pickles at an earlier time than usual. He was lying on his belly, in his open-ended tent, fast asleep with his head tucked under his wing.

"Good morning!" I said as Pickles snapped his head toward me and exclaimed, "What are you DOING?" Lights off!" I dropped the cover and turned off his lamp, deciding to let him sleep but knowing full well that he was too nosy to go back to bed.

As I puttered around making coffee I could hear "Want out" every few seconds and at first he was quiet and polite because his last episode kind of back fired, but gradually he grew louder and kept up until I lifted his cover and unlocked his cage. "Want breakfast, Bugger Brat!" he demanded as he climbed out in a huff but by the time he got to his outside perch he was in a better mood and eager to make up for his short behavior. "Good morning Bee! Give me little kiss." (He has called me Bee for a few years now – seldom Mommy or Mama anymore) I picked him up, kissed his beak and off we went to fix his breakfast.

After breakfast, I took him for a walk around the house on my hand and we stopped at all the windows along the way for a different perspective of the yard and neighborhood. We were chatting about the birds outside when suddenly, Pickles noticed a crow that was soaring above the house and blurted, "A pie in the sky!" It took me a moment to realize he was trying to repeat the exclamation I use each time I see a flying crow, which is 'There's a crow, up high in the sky!' I should really start enunciating more clearly.

While speaking to a lady on the lake trail during a walk with Neeka Dog on a leash and Pickles in his birdie backpack, Pickles kept cocking his head at her, peering into her face and repeating, "Biskalop". To this day, I still have no idea what he was trying to say or if this was just a word he made up but he still utters it now and then.

111

Later in the day, I watched him trying to sneak down from his cage to check out some food he had thrown on the floor earlier and just as he was reaching the bottom, he hollered, "Get back up!" and scrambled back up the bars. The dope is always doing this; ratting on himself and ruining his own fun.

About an hour before supper, Neil and I were trying to decide what to give him for s-u-p-p-e-r, spelling it so Pickles didn't hear and get all excited but his head snapped around to ask, "Supper? Supper time?"

For supper, Pickles got squash and cauliflower while we ate chicken salad sandwiches. I almost choked on mine when Pickles asked, "Got a bird in yer beak?" That one had to be a fluke, but an amusing one.

After dinner, to top the day off, a woman stopped by to drop off some things for a friend and when she glanced over at Pickles, who was sitting with one leg tucked up, she said, "Oh, poor birdie, what happened?" and before I could answer, Pickles piped up with, "Scary". "Scary?" asked the lady, "What's scary?" "Neeka" Pickles answered. The woman looked at me in shock – not because she'd just had a conversation with a bird but to say, "Oh my God. Did your dog do that to him?" "Of course not" I said, "Pickles' leg is fine" and to prove it, I had him step up on my hand.

It doesn't really matter what he comprehends and what is coincidence, it's amazing that he even says these things.

*I have a wonderful surprise for you, Pickles. Is it juice, Mom? Even more wonderful than that, Pickles. Oh my God, Mom – is it a barrel of juice and a*

112

*snorkel?? Cuz, like, anything less than that will be a huge disappointment now, Mom. You just HAVE to ruin everything, don't you, Pickles? Is this your way of saying you don't have a barrel of juice and a snorkel for me, Mom? Yes, Pickles. Then I will accept nothing less than a sack of potatoes, Mom. How about a French fry, Pickles? Oh my God, Mom – BEST surprise EVER!*

## What Kinda Bird?

Pickles has always been a very vocal bird and quick to learn new words and phrases. When he was three months old, he could already say things like, "Hello", "Peekaboo", "What are you doing" and "Want a snack". For the next few years, his vocabulary grew and when I stopped counting and keeping track of all his words, he was well over 100. Then, when he was about 8 years old (he is 10 at the time of this writing) he decided he wasn't going to learn any more words and instead, he was going to copy every sound he could. This included every wild bird in the neighborhood (dozens), each neighbor's dog's bark (several) and every sound he heard from the TV – mostly from commercials and especially electronic sounds. He still used his words, especially when he wanted something, but he dropped most of the rest of his vocabulary. Even during the years that he talked a lot, he would still drop some words and phrases for months or even a couple of years then suddenly pick it up again.

Then, after two years of very few new words and just as we had decided that was about it for his vocabulary, he started coming up with new words and phrases. It drove me crazy when he kept repeating something silly sounding and, after a few days, I finally figured out what he was saying. Sometimes,

113

when I was cold, I would say, "brrrrrr, it's cold isn't it Pickles?" and I am constantly looking at him and asking, "What are you up to, Pickles?" He had decided to put it together, run the words altogether as one and came up with, "Brrrrrrwhaddayupta" with the emphasis on UP. But, a few days after I figured out what he was saying, he stopped saying it. It will come back though, some day.

He has made up his own names for Neil and I. He used to call me Mommy or Mama when he was very young but then suddenly, and I have no idea why, he started calling me Bea. He's been doing it for about 8 years now and seldom calls me anything else, except for maybe Ratbugger or Buggerbutt and other sweet pet names. A few months ago, he got in the habit of calling me Mombum but forgot about it after a couple of weeks, maybe because I would ignore him when he did. Sometimes I wonder if Neil teaches him these things when I'm not around.

For Neil, he has always alternated between Neil and Daddy (except for the period he decided he liked Daddyburraddy) but recently he has mostly dropped 'Neil' and has altered 'Daddy' to 'Doddy'. If Pickles were talking to Neil, it would be 'Doddy' but if he was calling Neil and wanting some attention, it became, "Doddy, oddy, yoddy!" Every time he does it I want to break out in a singsong of, "Doddy, oddy, oxen free!" as in the children's game of hide-and-go-seek where they yell, "Ollie, ollie, oxen free!" to indicate that players who are hiding can come out in the open without losing the game. I imagine it's just a matter of time before Pickles adds the 'oxen free'.

114

Neil and I spend a lot of time sitting in the yard, or sitting in our rockers in the diningroom, staring out the windows at the pond and all the wild birds. We have planted over 100 trees and shrubs that provide food and shelter for the birds but mostly they come for the water, to bathe and drink. There are dozens of different kinds of birds that visit so we always have bird books handy so that we can identify them but before we look them up, you will often hear one of us pointing out a bird and asking the other if they know what it is.

I was puttering around one morning when I heard Neil ask me about a bird and I said, "I don't know, I didn't see it". "See what?" he asked. "The bird" I answered. "What bird?" he asked. "Didn't you just ask me, *what kind of bird is that?*?" I asked him. "No" he said, "You're hearing things". I looked over at Pickles, who was hanging around on his diningroom ropes, and he looked back at me and said, "What kind of bird is that?" Awesome!

He kinda blew it though, cognizant wise, when later that day we went for a walk around the lake, Pickles in his birdie backpack, and a man stopped to talk to Pickles. "Say 'hi' to the nice man, Pickles", I said. Pickles cocked his head at him and asked, "What kind of bird is that?"

*I found Mom's kitchen scissors while I was hanging out on the kitchen table. I know I'm not allowed to have them so I snatched them up and ran like hell across the table. When I got to the end of the table, I couldn't stop and I slid right off the edge and the weight of the scissors carried me straight down to the floor. Let that be a lesson to me about running with scissors ... until next time.*

## What a Day

From the moment I uncovered Pickles in the morning, he wouldn't stop talking about going to the aviary. While I was trying to drink my coffee and wake up, Pickles wasn't interested in his usual morning routine, or even his breakfast. "Wanna go in the aviary. Let's go to the aviary. Wanna go to the aviary ....", so I finally gave up, packed him up in his travel cage and transported him to the aviary. I thought to myself, *well, this is actually quite nice* as I sat in the sunshine, staring at the yard and pond and drank my coffee while listening to the pretty bird songs. Just as I was totally relaxed and thinking how thankful I was to Pickles for this great idea, he started squawking and insisting on going home. "Wanna go home. Want breakfast. Wanna go home. Let's go!"

I didn't want to go home so I figured I would play waitress and bring his breakfast to the aviary to eat. While he was running through his ropes and perches to reach it, I sat back down in my lawn chair. As I reached for my coffee, the squawking and demands began again. I was never going to get any peace and quiet this way so I packed him and his breakfast back inside to his cage. He immediately dove into his breakfast. Why he wouldn't eat it outside if he was so bloody hungry, I have no idea. Back to the computer and my coffee.

"WANNA GO IN THE AVIARY, WANNA GO IN THE AVIARY, WANNA GO IN THE AVIARY!!" Oh. My. GOD! I walked up to his cage, glared at him and said, "You've GOT to be kidding!" The LOOK he gave me! He was furious that I was taking such an attitude with him. He glared back at me as he crouched low and splayed his wings as if he was

116

going to lunge right into my face. Of course, he would never do such a thing – at least, he's never tried such a thing – but I figured what the heck, let's humour the guy. But, instead of taking him out to the aviary, I packed him up in his birdie backpack, grabbed Neeka Dog and his leash and off we went for a quick walk around the lake. Maybe that would shut him up.

As usual, it wasn't long before someone stopped to talk to us. A woman stood talking to Pickles and Pickles flattered her by giving her the wolf whistle and saying, "Hello, baby" in his sexy voice. It's hard to have a proper conversation with someone, or see how they are reacting or what they are doing sometimes because the backpack is on my back, of course, so I like it when people stand to the side of me but still, I have to crane my neck to be part of the circle. Sometimes I will take the backpack off and set it down on a nearby stump, bench or picnic table but that wasn't an option on that particular part of the trail and the woman stood where I couldn't see her while she talked to Pickles.

It wasn't my intention to stand there long and I was just waiting for a break in the conversation to politely carry on down the trail when suddenly she cried out, "OW!" and I knew immediately that the stupid woman had poked her finger through the bars, much to Pickles delight who obviously chomped down on it. I turned quickly but not quick enough to avoid the quick slap on the cage that the woman gave in reaction to her pain. I realize it was an unintended reaction on her part but I was furious. After a few choice words, I turned on my heel and walked away.

I was fuming as I walked on down the trail but had calmed down a bit by the time we met up with another woman a few minutes later. This woman told

117

me she had an African Grey just like Pickles but that it only liked her husband and I told her that Pickles had stopped liking Neil for a while but that we had fixed that. She asked for advice on how they could change it too so I started telling her all the things she could try and the things that had helped us. Each time, before I could finish, the lady was nodding impatiently saying, "Yeah, yeah, we tried that, what else?" and being quite short and rude about it. I could tell that she really hadn't tried the things I was suggesting and even asked a few trick questions to find out for sure but it was obvious that she was just looking for an easy fix. I was already in a very bad mood from the previous lady so I was getting very angry with this woman – not just because she was wasting my time and being rude but because I knew her parrot was suffering with an idiot like this for an owner.

I'd finally had enough of her attitude and as I turned to leave I said, "Well, ma'am. If you have, in fact, tried everything to change things and it didn't work, you really have to stop and wonder why your bird doesn't like you and, to be honest, it's perfectly clear to me."

She was pretty much speechless as I walked away but managed to say, "Excuse me?" to my back but I kept walking. I'm not a violent person but today I could have easily decked both these women. My day has been ruined and I'm taking deep breaths in an attempt to keep my anger at bay. I'm trying to stay patient with Neeka as he keeps stopping to sniff at things on the trail – something he doesn't normally do – so I keep asking him if he has to poop. While we are stopped one of those times that I'm waiting for Neeka, TWO ladies appear. One carries on down the trail while the other pauses to look at Pickles and before she can open her mouth to speak, Pickles shouts, "Do you hasta poop?" I'm giggling to myself and as I turn slightly to

118

see her reaction, Pickles decides that perhaps she needs some encouragement and maybe a promise of a reward so he says, "Poop for a snack!"

The lady says, "How funny!" and carries on down the trail, laughing, to catch up to her friend and I realize I have a big grin on my face. That bird snapped me right out of my bad mood and cheered me up for the rest of the day.

*I have a question for you, Mom. Sure, what is it, Pickles. (Poops down Mom's leg while sitting on her knee) Would you call that olive green or forest green?*

Pickles doesn't fly much - he prefers to walk - however, he flies very well when he decides to do so because he was allowed to fledge when he was a baby, before his first wing clip. He can hover in one spot, he banks well and he lands easily on an extended hand (or anywhere else) with pin point precision – except when he's startled. When he's startled, he flies like a big, stupid moth or an out of control ping pong ball careening off one thing just to fly blindly in to the next. You just shake your head at the completely senseless panic he suffers over nothing, and before he has time to process it.

Having a slightly timid little Min Pin dog just adds to the situations like when a huge piece of clear plastic blew off the garden and flew past the patio doors in the diningroom while Neeka lay in the sun in front of the windows and Pickles preened on his ropes. Pickles may not have even noticed had it not been for Neeka's terror and sudden barking, and I don't know which scared him most but it sent him flying straight into the new roll of carpet that was standing on it's end on the kitchen table. This was the same carpet he'd been mortally afraid of for the past two days and why, even in his fright, he would choose to fly into that – the scariest object in the whole house – I have no idea. Did I mention 'moth'? Like a moth to the flame. Straight into the jaws of danger and possible death.

Of course, the carpet just doubled his terror as he bounced off it, making a bee line for the top of the fridge, sending all the boxes of dog cookies crashing to the ground, scaring him flying to the dishwasher, sliding across the surface like an out-of-control plane on the tarmac, grabbing Dad's set of keys in hopes of something stationary stopping him from shooting off the edge but they just carried along with him, sliding straight on to a pantry shelf where he probably would have been fine if the sound of the keys crashing into the recycling pail below him didn't cause him to fly straight up, head first in the shelf above him then panicking him into thinking he was trapped and then finally being rescued by Dad, who had been trying to catch up with Pickles the whole time. Pickles stepped up on Neil's hand, raised his wings and fluffed his feathers all nonchalant-like and pretended like he'd meant to do all that.

When Pickles had originally taken off with a loud flourish, Neeka was caught off guard and assumed he was also being attacked from the rear but his retreat was impeded by the fact that he was running in place like a cartoon character on the tiled floor. However, it was only a couple of short moments before fright turned to delight at cookies raining from the sky.

The same friggin' day, Neil decided to roll Pickles' cage outside so that he could spray it with a hose, scrub it down and then leave it in the sun to dry. He tried to get Pickles to step up to take him to another play area but Pickles wouldn't budge. Neil tried to explain to Pickles that he had to get off the cage because we all know how scared he gets when his cage moves beneath him but he wouldn't listen. Neil rolled the cage a tiny bit, just to warn Pickles what was about to happen and that's all it took. Off he went, flying like a maniac, straight into his Get-A-Grip Net and tangled like a fly in a spider web.

*OMG! OMG! OMG! Today, while Mom had her back turned, I climbed down from my cage and went for a little walkabout. First I stopped and investigated the cranny between the fridge and the counter and then I*

*scattered dog food out of Neeka Dog's bowl all over the kitchen floor and*
*then I headed down the hallway, knocking on all the closed doors until I*
*ended up in Mom and Dad's room. Mom left the door open on her bedside*
*table, obviously for me to play in, so I climbed inside and I found a mask,*
*whip and handcuffs! OMG – you know what this means? My mom's a*
*Superhero!*

## You Talkin' To Me?

Another typical conversation around here while everyone's doing their own
thing around the house and calling to each other …

Pickles: You talking to me?

Mom: I didn't say anything.

Dad: You talking to me?

Mom: Yes, I just answered you.

Dad: I didn't ask you anything.

Mom: Oh. I thought you asked if I was talking to you.

Dad: Nope.

Pickles: Are you talking to me?

Dad: All I said was, "Nope".

Mom:  What?  Are you talking to me?

Dad:  All I said was, "All I said was, 'Nope'."

Mom:  Stop talking to me.

Dad:  Sure.

Pickles:  Are you talking to me?

Dad:  All I said was, "Sure"!  Jeez – I'm not talking to you anymore!

Pickles:  What?

Silence.  They're both fed up with each other and aren't speaking anymore.

Pickles:  I'm hungry.

*Mom, I'd really like some pudding on a spoon.  Okay, Pickles – here ya go, some nice plum pudding.  Thanks, Mom – Wow, look how far that spoon flew and how nice purple looks on our yellow walls.  Pickles! – I can't believe you would lie to me like that ... saying you want pudding, just so you can throw it across the room.  Really, Mom? – Cuz that's like, all I live for.*

<u>Juice</u>

Pickles loves juice, especially grape juice. He likes apple juice now and then, depending on the type, and calls it "appo juice". I like grape juice so we always have it around but Pickles doesn't get it that often, even though he asks for it all the time, because of the high sugar content – especially if he's already been eating grapes.

He was driving me crazy for months when he started calling everything, 'juice'. I'd say, "Want some banana?" He'd say, "Juice". I'd say, "No, it's banana". I'd offer him a walnut and he'd say, "Juice!" and I'd tell him, "No, this is a walnut". It didn't matter what I offered him, he'd say, "Juice!" But then it finally dawned on me. This had become his word for showing pleasure. It's like, "Cool, man!" Or, "Awesome!" Somewhere along the way, he decided that juice was so wonderful that just the word alone indicated how wonderful other things could be.

It's become a saying around our house now. If Neil or I think something is cool we say, "That's juice, man!" Or, "How juice is THAT, eh?"

*Pickles! You ate a bunch of my lunch, walked all through it with your dirty little feet and threw half of it on the table, chairs and floor! Oh sorry, Mom – I thought you gave it to me and just set it over there.*

### Squawk!

I was chatting to Pickles while making up a new birdie bread and just as I said, "Pickles, I'm making you a new …" he piped up with a loud, "Squawk!" then looked at me as if to say, "Sorry, Mom. What were you saying?" So I said, "Well, Pickles, I was just trying to tell you that I'm …."

And he let out a louder, "Squawwwwk!" then stopped, cocked his head and looked at me with a kind of shocked look as if thinking, "Oh my God, not sure how that happened again, Mom, but please continue. "Jeez, Pickles, I just wanted to let you know that …" "SQUAWWWWWWWWK!" Then he looked at me, all smug and all, as if to say, "Sorry, Mom. I think this will just have to wait until you stop being so bloody boring."

This behaviour wasn't new. This is Pickles' rude way of telling us to shut up, that he doesn't want to listen to us anymore. Kind of like a spoiled little kid plugging their ears with their fingers and shouting, "Blah, blah, blah, blah, blah" so they can't hear what you're saying.

*Mom had a friend over and they were having coffee and biscotti but Mom had to leave the room to answer the phone so I decided to jump over to the table and help myself to a piece of her friend's biscotti and she shooed me away with her hand just as I was about to land! I turned with a loud squawk and landed back on my playstand, all mad and muttering and stuff. I had settled down by the time Mom walked in and said, "Pickles, what did you do??" So I gave her my sweet, innocent face and told her, "Nothing, Mom. I was a complete delight!" Then the Biscotti Bag ratted me out and I was removed from the room. But I got what I wanted – peace and quiet and a piece of biscotti dropped in my dish. Take that, Biscotti Bag Lady!*

# Who Let the Dogs Out?

Pickles is not very good at singing whole songs and will often mix two or three songs or phrases into the original. When he sings Raffi's 'Banana Phone' it comes out, "Ring, ring, ring, ring, ring, ring, ring, banana phone … answer the phone … hello? … boop boop". He gets sidetracked halfway through the song and has to answer the phone.

He gets sidetracked with 'Home, Home on the Range' too. Sometimes he'll sing the whole first line but he usually just sings, "Home, home … wanna go home? Let's go home, home …"

'Knick Knack Patty Whack, Give a Dog a Bone' is, "Knick knack, wanna snack". 'Row, Row, Row Your Boat' is, "Row row row, ho ho ho" (Santa Claus).

Pickles is always pretty quiet in the mornings while waiting to be uncovered. By quiet, I mean that he will talk to himself or practice his wild bird songs but he never makes a fuss about wanting out of his cage. It doesn't matter how long Neil and I want to sleep, Pickles will wait politely.

This particular morning, Pickles got tired of his bird songs and switched to a yappy little dog and barked, "arf, arf, arf" until we got up and uncovered him. As soon as the cage door was opened, he climbed out and sat on the top of the cage and started barking like a big dog, "woof, woof, woof" and then started practicing his new song, "Who Let the Dogs Out?" He can't say the whole thing though, he can only sing, "Who Goes Out?" And, when he asks a question like that, he has to answer and this morning he sang, "Who Goes

126

Out? Daddy go. Be right back. Woof, woof, woof woof".

*Mom was wrapping books to ship and I wanted to help but she wouldn't let me. Finally, I reached for the tape and tried to pull a piece off but I wasn't strong enough so Mom cut the piece I was holding with my beak. It wasn't so much fun after all, it stuck to my beak, my feet and my feathers and everything and made it hard to play with. Mom laughed and when she tried to get the tape off me, I used my beak to staple myself to her hand. She had to rewrap the books cuz of the blood but I think I made my point, and that is ... staples hurt more than tape.*

## Breakfast, Lunch and Supper But No Snack

Pickles usually gets peas or corn for breakfast but one morning Neil whipped up scrambled eggs and Pickles got some in his bowl. He has a pink hanging toy on top of his cage and he likes to sit next to it, coo at it, talk to it, rub his head lovingly on it, bang his beak and regurgitate for it. We call it his girlfriend and the minute Pickles discovered delicious scrambled eggs in his bowl, he swallowed as much as he could, as fast as he could and ran up to the top of his cage to regurgitate the egg for his girlfriend. I tossed a piece of multigrain toast in his bowl and he sprinted down, grabbed it and took it up to his girlfriend too. It was incredibly sweet and the most romantic meal EVER.

For lunch, Pickles got oatmeal and banana, all mashed together. He loves this but perhaps he wasn't all that hungry after the eggs and toast because instead, he climbed up on the rim of the bowl, reached one talon down and started squeezing the mash between his toes. Then he did it with the other

127

foot. Next thing I knew, he had managed to get both feet inside and was stomping around the bowl like he was mashing grapes for wine. After he was finished, he tracked mashed banana and oatmeal all over his perches and cage bars.

That evening's conversation:

Pickles: Want some supper.

Me: Soon.

Pickles: Want some supper!

Me: Dad will get it for you after he makes OUR supper.

Pickles: Daddy eat supper?

Me: Yes.

Pickles: Daddy burp beans?

Me: Don't be rude, Pickles!

Pickles: WANT SUPPER, DAMMIT!

A few minutes after supper, I got up to get Pickles his nighttime snack of an almond in the shell but as I walked past his cage he hollered, "I don't wanna snack!" He obviously got his words mixed up but I obeyed and sat back down on the couch, just to teach him a lesson.

*Stupid Mom. Dad went out of town, she forgot yesterday was Halloween and was planning on buying candy today. By the time she realized it was Halloween yesterday, she was lying on the couch in her PJ's with no make-up and a splitting headache and couldn't go to the store so she closed all the curtains and shut off most of the lights and pretended she wasn't home. But while it was still daylight, people kept knocking on our door so I kept yelling out to people, loud enough that they could hear me. Mostly, I called out, "Anybody home?" and "Mama's home!" and "Daddy's home!" and "Pickles' home!" and "Want some supper?" and then I'd wolf whistle as loud as I could. I did all this to rat Mom out and watch her cringe and die inside. And also for the benefit of her headache.*

## Pickles' Pumpkin Oatmeal Cookies

I came up with this recipe one day when I had some pumpkin left over after making people cookies last fall. Pickles absolutely LOVES them, which is great because it's a healthy snack that I can give him every day.

½ cup of mashed pumpkin. You can use either mashed, canned, plain pumpkin or you can mash the insides of a fresh one.

1 cup of oatmeal – uncooked

1 beaten egg

¼ cup walnuts. I break them up into really small pieces.

129

1/3 pomegranate, with juice. Just scoop out the pomegranate seeds, saving all the juice that comes out of it.

Extra pomegranate seeds for topping.

Put all the ingredients in a bowl and mix well. You want the texture to be like cookie dough basically. Add more oatmeal if you need to make it drier or add more juice or some water if it's too dry.

Lightly grease a cookie sheet and then drop them by the spoon full. For mine, I used about a teaspoon. Depending on the size of your bird, you might want to make them bigger or smaller. The size you see going in, is the size that comes out.

Push one Mountain Ash berry into the top of each cookie. It doesn't matter what you use on top. If you used fresh pumpkin, use a raw pumpkin seed. Or a cheerio, piece of fruit or a berry, nut or anything else your bird would like

Bake in the oven at 350 F for about 12 minutes. Watch them as your times may vary. I live in a high altitude area so cooking times may be different for you. Also, the size of the cookie you make may slightly vary the cooking time.

Let them cool a bit on the cookie sheet then place the whole sheet in the freezer for an hour or two. Remove the cookies and place them in baggies and freeze. Putting the cookies and cookie sheet in the freezer will harden them so they won't stick together in a big mass after you put them in baggies for freezing.

## Banana Sandwiches

I was making myself a peanut butter sandwich one day and Pickles was watching me through the kitchen/livingroom window hollering, "Want some!" so I sliced off a couple of round banana pieces, put peanut butter in between and stuck a cheerio on the top. He was in 7th Heaven.

## Corn Cob Hanging Toy

Someone gave us a mess of local corn last summer and I knew we'd never eat it all so I decided to fix it up for Pickles. In the fall, you can always find those little dried corncobs in the produce section – the plain dried ones, not the decorative ones that have been treated – and Pickles loves to chew on, and toss, the corn kernels. It keeps him nice and busy. So, I took a few of the cobs, pulled the husks off – but left them fastened at the top – pulled the threads off, washed the cobs and set them in our cold room to dry and forgot about them.

I guess it was a couple of months later that I pulled them out, fastened leather strips to the top (the husks enabled me to do that) and hung them for Pickles. They are naturally dried so he will eat some too but mostly he rips the kernels off and tosses them. When he's done, I save the individual husks for wrapping treats for foraging. The corncobs make a great food toy and very cheap if you're buying the cobs. You can also hang them fresh, cooked or raw. BUT, we live in a very dry climate so things like this dry up instead of rotting or molding so don't try this in damper climates. You could make them in a food dehydrator though.

Skewers

I've talked about this before and always post on Facebook but it's worth repeating because it's so effective for getting your bird to eat fruit and veggies that he doesn't like. You can buy hanging skewers made for parrots – just Google 'parrots, skewers' to find them – or you can string the produce on clean rope, SS chain or leather strip (not too long if it's thin rope/string that could wrap around a bird's foot or neck). Just cut a variety of fruit or veggies into chunks and string them altogether. Make sure to include a couple of things he does like too. This will keep him busy and entertained and even if he doesn't like some of the items, he will probably bite them all off, piece by piece and toss them while getting some nutrients in his mouth and hopefully get used to the taste and eventually start liking some of it. I like hanging a whole pumpkin or squash (small ones) seeds and all.

## That's it for me. Pickles will now take over ...

*A man came over to give Mom and Dad an estimate on doing some renovations on the house and Neeka Dog and I barked and barked and barked at him to warn Mom and Dad of the danger. Neeka barked right in front of him and the man wanted to know where the other dog was cuz I was barking from the livingroom. He was surprised and thought it was funny that I was barking. I don't know why because, like, how else do you warn of danger and scare people away – chirp like a bird?*

*Mom, stop spraying me with water just to make me stop plucking my chest! Water is evil and the side effects are, that it doesn't work at all.*

*I was looking at the nice, black bananas sitting on the counter and asked Mom for some. She said 'no' and told me that the darker they are, the more sugar content and that it would put me over my sugar limit so she's going to use them to make banana bread. Curses! I think that woman has a black heart to match the black bananas but apparently we'll never know for sure – not without an autopsy. I tried to book one for her but I found out you have to be dead for that. Rules, rules, rules.*

*Last weekend we went to a really nice lake and mom thought it was so beautiful and peaceful that she told dad she'd like to be buried there. I don't know why he didn't do it right then and there, now he's missed his chance.*

*I stole 7 yummy grapes. Mom got mad and told me it's too much sugar for one little bird. I told her – in dog grapes, I only had one.*

*If you bite someone in the forest, does anybody scream?*

*I like chasing people who are scared of birds. I keep chasing them, making them run all over the place and when I catch up to them I say, "Sorry, I thought you were someone else."*

*I went to bed in my cage and after I was covered up I realized I was hungry for a nice snack so I called out "Mom! I want a walnut!" She told me, "No way. You go to sleep". I said, "MOM! I really, really want a walnut!" and she said, "Go to sleep before I come in there and wring your bloody neck!"*

*I said, "Mom, when you come to wring my neck, could you bring a walnut?"*

*Mom said I had to have a bath today and I told her – no way, I just had one this morning! She said I definitely did NOT. Rats. I must be thinking of a different morning.*

*Mom's friend came to visit with the baby again. I'm glad mom doesn't make me wear diapers like him. It must be hard to run away from your mom with a steaming turd between your legs.*

*I have this annoying squawk that I use when I want mom's attention. I used it today while she was reading on the couch and she got up and left the room. She does that cuz she thinks she's using some kinda psychology on me and figures that will teach me a lesson. But really, that's what I wanted all along. As soon as she left the room, I was singing and whistling and happy as a lark. You can't beat ME at psychology.*

*What did I just ask for, Mom? That's right, a snack. And what is this crap you just handed me? No, give your head a shake, this is NOT a snack, this is a piece of crap. Since when have I ever eaten crap and since when did you stop caring about your fingers?*

*Mom, I just lost 2 of my beautiful red butt feathers! I'm busy baking, Pickles. Mom, the dog got them!! Pickles, I'm too busy baking cookies to worry about that right now. Mom, how can you think about cookies when I'm falling to pieces and the dog is eating my body parts?!!!! The cookies are for you, Pickles – and they're made of Cheerios. Oooooo, gimme!*

*I have never bothered to learn the smoke alarm. Maybe cuz I hardly ever heard it, I dunno, but lately the new one's been going off a lot more so I decided to copy it – just as loud. If I had known how much it hurt Mom's ears, I'd have been doing it years ago.*

*Can I have some apple, Mom?*
*Mmmm*
*I'm really hungry, Mom.*
*Mmmm*
*I'd really like some apple.*
*Mmmm*
*Are you listening to me?*
*Mmmm*
*Apple, please.*
*Mmmm*
*Mom, I just chewed a hole in the ceiling.*
*What did you do that for??!!*
*To get your attention, Mom. But, in hindsight, I doubt that was the right thing to do for some apple.*

*For crying out loud, Pickles, why do you keep finding ways to annoy me? Why is it that tossing things around, making a mess, chewing and destroying things I care about is so bloody interesting to you? What is it that I'm missing here? I dunno, Mom – maybe an elevated blood-alcohol content? Chill out, eh.*

*Oh, Pickles, Christmas is coming – the time to open your heart. Awesome, Mom – can I use a can opener on yours?*

*Mom, I hate to be a needy bird, a demanding bird and your bird, but where the hell is my lunch?? It's in your bowl, Pickles. No, it's not, Mom – I'm sitting on the rim, looking into it and there is no food in here. It's in your outside cage bowl, Pickles. Awesome – dining on the patio!*

*I was sitting on the couch with mom while she was eating chips and guacamole and I said, "Want some" and mom started to hand me a chip with a bit of dip when she suddenly remembered that avocado is toxic to me. I was really, really mad cuz she had that chip right in my face before she snatched it away. I yelled at her, "Want some, want some, WANT SOME!" and she told me no way cuz it might kill me. I don't believe it. You think you know EVERYTHING mom but your name is not GOOGLE!*

*Mom fed me stupid broccoli today. She says it's healthy and good for me and I'm sure it is, but at what cost?*

*Mom says Neeka the Dog always seems to be humping a stuffy toy but I think he's trying to jump over it and he's just too small to make it.*

*Mom! Neeka the dog is trying to eat his dick!*
*He's not eating it, he's cleaning it – she said.*
*Oh. Well, if he's not gonna eat it, can I have it?*

*Whenever I do the 'Grey Lean', away from something that's scary while I'm on Dad's hand, he calls me a chicken and goes 'brawk, brawk, brawk'. I've already been doing the chicken sound for years so now I started beating him to the punch and whenever I get scared of something, I yell out, 'brawk,*

*brawk, brawk'. At Christmas, Dad tried to put me near the turkey before they cooked it and I said, "Scary! Brawk, brawk, brawk!" I'm a chicken that's ascared of a turkey!*

*Mom put some scary looking cottage cheese curds in my bowl! What is this?? Fear Factor???*

*I was sitting on mom's good hand but couldn't resist jumping over to her broken arm sling cuz it's so much fun to play on and the only way Mom could get me off it was to open my favorite hall closet and stick her arm in there so I would jump off and play there instead. Then she closed the door. Apparently, by virtue of my actions, I was being punished. HAHAHAHAHAHAHAHAHA!!*

*I was going to do something really nice for Mom today but then something shiny caught my eye.*

*We went for a walk around the lake today. The lake is right in town, which is why our town is called, Logan Lake. We ran into people along the way but today I didn't talk except for when Mom told me to say 'hi' to a nice man. The rest of the time, all I did was laugh at kids when they stopped to look at me. I find children hilarious. When we were on the forest trail, it upset me that I couldn't see Neeka Dog. Neeka always walks beside us where I can see him but the trail is narrow at times so mom would let him walk in front. Because I'm on Mom's back, I don't know this and I can't see him so I hasta call him all the time so I do little kissy sounds and quick whistles to call him. Mom didn't appreciate this because Neeka would stop mid-trail and almost trip her. I spent a lot of time chewing the canvas on the backpack but it doesn't help because I can't chew through the bars to escape. Mom tried to get me to talk to one couple but all I did was bark at them. "Is that all you can do, is bark?" the man asked me. I thought that was a silly question so I cawed. When we got home, mom found the potato chip that someone had snuck in the cage for me. I ate some of it and was saving the rest for later but Mom stole it from me with the excuse that it had too much salt for me. Way to punctuate the end of a great day, Mom.*

*Here Pickles, I found a new broccoli dish that might help you to start liking broccoli – how does it taste? Oh My God, Mom – it tastes like I'm gonna die!*

*OMG, Mom, it's scary when the power goes out and there's no light! ACK – what was that sound?! You pooped on the newspaper below you, Pickles. OMG, my poop is epic even in the dark!*

*You may have yelled at me to 'Get back up!' when I climbed down from my cage and almost hit the floor, Mom, but yelling at me didn't make me get back up – I was heading that way anyway because that piece of lettuce I was going for turned out to be just my poop and I wasn't THAT hungry.*

*I'm sorta sorry that I tossed that toast and jam onto the TV screen but it's your own fault. When you offered it to me the first time, didn't you hear the look I gave you?*

*Why did I chew a hole in the curtains, you ask? Because when I was hiding behind them I couldn't see through them and I needed a window to keep a lookout for you.*

138

*I will help you with supper tonight, Mom. I mean, I won't actually help cook it but I will help by letting you know when I'm hungry.*

*This is a delicious banana! I've never had such a delicious banana in my whole life, unless you count the thousands of delicious bananas I had before this one.*

*I tossed the bowl of nuts off the coffee table but I don't know why Mom's so uptight about it – she's the one that said how important it is to have regular bowl movements.*

*When I'm mad at somebody, I just draw their blood. That way, I get rid of my frustrations and it's like, no harm done.*

*Mom gave me a bunch of blackberries in my dish and I tossed them at the wall, one by one, until they were all gone. Mom picked them all up and wiped down the black spots on the wall and then took them all away. I yelled at her because I wanted some back because I never got a chance to eat any but she was teaching me a lesson or something and wouldn't give me any. It was all going great until it wasn't.*

*Mom, pick up my piece of pineapple, will ya? I thought you threw it because you didn't like it, Pickles. No, I like it fine, Mom, I did it on mistake. (Mom fetches the pineapple and I bite her finger as she hands it to me) What did you do THAT for, Pickles! Cuz I can, Mom. Cuz I can.*

*I noticed Neeka Dog's toy on the floor near my cage – his pop bottle full of beads that make such a racket when he plays with it – so I climbed down to play with it myself. It was heavy but I kept picking it up with my beak and dropping it on the floor to make it rattle. To my surprise, Mom came in and found me with it. I didn't realize that she could hear the noise too – I thought that was just a 'bird' thing. Besides, I figured a woman of her advanced years is likely going deaf anyway. The dog probably ratted me out. He's a turd.*

*If I could only squeeze through that grate in the floor and get inside the vents, I would never be bored again.*

*My God, Mom! What takes you so long to get my snacks and make my meals?? I wait very patiently for about 3 seconds but my beak is still empty! What did you say? You don't like my tone? Well, I'd use a different tone but then how would you know that I'm mad at you?! Just bring me my food, old woman!*

*I got mad at mom cuz she wouldn't give me any of her potato chips and I called her a Rat Bugger. Dad said, "That wasn't very nice, Pickles. What if she died and that was the last thing you ever said to her?" I thought – OH NO! That would be horrible! The last thing to say to her should have been, "Where do you keep the sesame snaps?"*

*Mom tried to feed me broccoli again. I said, "What's this crap? I'm gonna throw it in your face!" "Go ahead. It won't hurt me," she answered. "Yeah?" I said, "Well, it will after I tie it to a brick!"*

*Mom was talking about this guy who's in his 30's and won't let go of his mom's apron strings. Ohhhh, snap! If mom wore an apron, I wouldn't either - I'd hang on those babies all day long!*

*As I sat on the kitchen counter with my wings practically glued to the counter top, I started to regret flying into the bowl of flour before landing in the sink of water.*

*Mom was wearing a new ring today and even though it was a cheapy, it was really nice and I wanted to share it so I snapped the stone out of the setting on the first try. Well!! Mom shouted out all kinds of words that would not go well with a halo if she wore one. What a trucker mouth.*

*It seems there is a limit to mom&dad's intelligence. I have learned all I can from them and am now seeking a new, smarter home with lots of cupboards and closets. Broccoli eaters need not apply. Please provide a picture of your snacks and remote controls.*

*Sometimes it can be fun to climb down my cage and sneak over to the kitchen table and bite mom's toe. I'm thinking of changing my name to Fart. Because I'm silent but deadly.*

*Mom, I want you to get me stuff because YOU want to, not because I want you to. I would never ask you to do something you don't want to do. Now, go get me a walnut. No, Pickles, I don't want to. Wait, Mom! Forget what I said – we both know I don't care what you want.*

*Okay, so I always throw stuff on the floor. And yes, sometimes you can tell that I didn't mean to throw something because I will do my whiney little, "ohhhh" so you will go get it and hand it to me. But by the time you do that, the game has changed and I have to throw it back on the floor. Because I like that grunt sound you old people make when you have to bend over.*

*Daddy was napping on the couch so I decided to fly over and join him. When I landed on him, he whisked me up, put me on the floor and yelled at me to 'Go Home!' so I head-bobbed and chicken-walked all the way back to my cage, all happy and stuff. I don't know why. I don't know why I was happy and I don't know why I actually obeyed a command when I was getting nothing out of it, but I'm hoping for a caramel. What did you say, Mom? It's Karma? I don't care, as long as it's delicious.*

*I kept calling mom in the room and then when she came, I just ignored her. She asked me if I ever heard the story about the little boy who cried wolf and when I just ignored her and didn't answer, she started rambling on about some stupid little boy. I just wanted her to shut up and go away but she kept droning on and on and on and I thought – Oh, what fresh hell is this? Finally she finished and I think some wolf got a nice snack or something, I don't really know for sure cuz I was only partially listening to the story but I didn't hear my name in it so it couldn't have been that good.*

*Mom says that if you put a drinking glass up to a wall and place your ear against it, you can hear people talking in the other room. I thought this was pretty cool, until I found out there actually has to BE people in the other room. What a rip.*

*Mom's always telling me what I can and can't do; it's like living with a dicktater. And even when she's not tatering, she's still a dick.*

*Well, it's bear season once again and they're roaming the neighborhood. Last night I heard mom outside in the yard yelling, "Bear! Help! Bear!" Yeah, right. Like a bear's gonna help her.*

*MOM! I have a stringy poop hanging outta my butt and it's chasing me everywhere! HELP! ... Are you laughing at me?? Stop it - it's not funny! Just shut up and wipe my butt!*

*I told Mom, "Mixing broccoli into my mashed bananas doesn't fool me, it just makes me start hating bananas because it tastes like broccoli." She told me, "Pickles, just eat what's in your bowl – it ain't gonna eat itself". Well, can ya BLAME it??*

*Mom, stop trying to scare me into eating all my vegetables. People who eat broccoli die every day too, ya know.*

*I think that a very good way to get out of eating broccoli for the rest of your life would be to take a bite, go limp and soil yourself.*

*Me: Stop spraying me!*
*Mom: You need to get wet – you stink.*
*Me: It's yourself you smell, not me.*
*Mom: No, you're the one who's dirty, not me.*
*Me: I like my dirt; it's probably the only thing holding me together.*
*Mom: Do as I say - I do not need a parrot arguing with me!*
*Me: And yet, you bought one.*

*I don't understand why mom won't let me do anything I want. I told her I have FB friends that would take me and they would let me do anything I want. She told me to get off my high horse and that I'm no more special than any other bird. I said – Oh yeah? What do you know? You're not special either, you don't even have hollow bones ... wait, I has a horse?*

*Pickles! Just look at the mess you've made all over the floor with your food and toys! You're always making so much work for me! Oh, Mom – I do just as much work around here, I just don't complain about it.*

*When I say "peek-a-boo" then duck behind something only as wide as my head, you can't say "I see you" because you CAN'T see me! If I can't see you, then you can't see me, so stop trying to ruin the game!*

*I had to go in my cage when mom's friend stopped by during her road trip through BC. She pulled something scary looking out of a cage and I couldn't stop staring at it and wondering what it was. Finally mom told me it's a hairless cat. How nice, I thought - now please go flush it.*

*When your mom stubs her toe in the other room and is screaming in pain? Start screaming yourself – scream like you just got your wing ripped off by a toy – scream bloody murder. It takes your mom's mind of her own little owie and let's her know that she can still walk. After she runs in to see if you're okay, she may not actually thank you but just know that you done a good thing.*

*Yes, mom. You heard right, I said damn it. And what do you know – who's voice did I say it in? That's right, yours. I think it's YOUR mouth that*

144

*should be washed out with soap, and mine with grape juice please.*

*Mom caught Dad and me in bed together! Dad was supposed to be working and I was supposed to be eating my lunch back at my cage but when mom left the computer room and walked through the house, neither of us were anywhere to be found. Finally, she looked in the bedroom and lifted the covers and the jig was up! We were having such a nice nap but she just has to ruin everything.*

*Oh, for cripes sake, Mom. So I threw that grape across the room, so what? Just because I've been saying, "Wanna Grape" for the past hour, doesn't necessarily mean I want to EAT one. Grapes are quite enjoyable in the mouth or flying through the air. Besides, I know you'll go fetch it for me and that I can still eat it any time I please. Now, fetch it up! Good guuuuurrrrrrlllllll!*

*Daddy was gone and Neeka Dog was lying on Mom's lap. I hollered, "Daddy's home!" and Neeka jumped up and hit mom's arm just as she was taking a drink of her pop and made her spill it everywhere. Dad wasn't really home but Neeka's so stupid, he went and sat on the back of the couch looking out the window for him. Mom said, "Neeka, why do you listen to that bloody bird?" then she looked at me and said, "Pickles, why do you always have to lie to the dog??" Isn't it obvious? Because I'm a parrot, and I can.*

*I was playing inside my snuggly when I happened to peer out and there was Mom's big fat face a few inches from mine – it scared the crap out of me! "Do you have a second, Pickles?" she asked. A second what? Poop?*

145

*What's wrong with the one you just scared out of me?*

*Pickles, can I ask you a question? Sure, Mom, as long as you're not fussy about the answer.*

*Dammit! I asked for a snack 15 minutes ago. Who do you have to regurgitate on to get a snack around here?*

*Mom: Pickles, what are all your little toys' eyeballs doing in your tent?*
*Me: Sometimes I get mad.*

*Thank God for Facebook, otherwise I'd have to call 3519 people and let them know I had perogies for lunch.*

*Dad has taught me some valuable lessons in life – Don't talk with your mouth full. Failure is only temporary, quitting is forever. It's okay to share your emotions. It's okay to march to the beat of a different drum. And to consider how stocks fit into your overall financial plan, and whether you should buy individual stocks, or buy them via mutual funds and that, from time to time, you will need to adjust your cost basis to account for return of capital, splits, depletion, spinoffs, distributions, etc.*

*"Thank you for stealing my toast and throwing it butter side down on the floor, Pickles".*
*"My pleasure, Mom!"*
*"My thank you wasn't sincere, Pickles".*
*"Yes, but my pleasure is!"*

*Mom gave me a turnip and no way I would eat it. I won't eat anything new unless I've tried it before.*

*I was sitting quietly on mom's knee and half asleep and then I turned my head and opened my eyes to look at mom, just as she stuck her finger out to scratch behind my ear, and she poked me in the eye and almost blinded me! I didn't get too upset though cuz I figure being blind is just as good as having sight, except with out the seeing part.*

*Mom happened to look at me through her reading glasses when she walked up to give me a snack and I think I had a seizure looking at those HUGE eyes! It really freaked me out and I practically fell off my perch! If I wore those reading glasses, my eyes would be bigger than my head which would probably make me look real surprised or scared or something, but also very cool.*

*Sometimes I like to hide behind a toy or something so mom gets scared and thinks I flew out the window or something. Mom's afraid it might give her a heart attack but if we look on the bright side, it might give her a heart attack.*

*I forgive you for getting upset when I snapped the arm off your glasses, Mom. Don't worry; I love you just the way I am.*

*Okay, I threw the spoon you were using to feed me warm rice with because I felt I deserved a bigger spoon with more rice but when you brought the rice to me in that huge ladle, well, it was just too darn scary and as much as I wanted all that rice it was holding, I just didn't have the nerve to come near that thing. Go back and get the small spoon now. Do not roll your eyes at me and please remember that you must adhere to all the rules that I make up on the spot.*

*~~~~~~~~ I know you all think I'm exaggerating when I tell you how mean mom is to me but after this, I'm sure you'll agree with me. Read on, my friends ...*

*It was a day in hell with her yesterday – she replaced the paper on the bottom of my cage with no thought as to how much effort I put into my well-shaped poop piles, or that I might prefer dried up brown bananas and rock hard corn mixed with cage debris. She took my dirty water bowl and didn't care that I was suddenly thirsty as hell and almost died of dehydration in the 45 seconds it took her to bring me fresh stuff.*

*Then she had the nerve to turn on the stereo instead of my TV, assuming that I would rather listen to music. Sure, it turned out she was right about that but I had to endure my own temper tantrum till I realized that and then found myself singing and whistling ... I thought I was still yelling at her but realized I was actually singing to the music. So yeah, the whole thing was pretty stressful for me.*

*I wanted pudding for lunch, even asked for it specifically and ever so politely, but is that what I got? Noooo. She insisted that pudding lunches were not very healthy for me, that she loved me too much to kill me with bad nuturition, so instead, she gave me porridge. I mean what kind of mom DOES that?? And don't forgive her just because she mixed in some banana and a couple of drops of delicious Canadian Maple Syrup – and the fact that I devoured every morsel in what would be considered Olympics record time – the fact remains that she did not give me what I asked for which, in my*

148

*opinion, should be punishable by death or a reasonable facsimile.*

*So anyway, I know you are sitting there wondering how I have been able to endure this type of treatment all day every day, for almost 10 years – and I know that as horrific as this all sounds, it's difficult to read this without looking away, but of course, you can't look away when you're reading – not without missing something. But as bad as it's been to read so far, it's only going to get worse. Look away, those with faint hearts.*

*Soon after the lunch ordeal, she decided to take me for a fun walk around the house – an adventure of fun and discovery that lasted close to an hour – but refused to let me play in the linen closet! Just because I've chewed holes in too many nice things and have now decided that the doorframe needs my personal decorating touch???*

*Then, on the return trip down the hall, I grabbed for the linen closet doorknob as mom walked by and knocked myself clean off her hand and down to the floor. I tried to hang on to the knob but it's round and smooth and not the least bit bird-friendly. Regardless, mom should be anticipating my every move and she should have made sure I didn't fall but she didn't so therefore she placed me directly in the path of danger and God only knows what painful death I barely avoided with my cat-like reflexes and ability to land on my feet. I'm sure child/pet/family or any other kind of welfare, would be very interested in such goings-on around here. But wait, there's more.*

*I wanted to sit on the back of the couch and she obliged but it was just a ruse because there wasn't a damn thing happening outside that might hold my interest so I chomped a couple of holes in the curtains to fend off my boredom and, quick as a wink I was nabbed and transported back to my cage* where some new hanging toys were waiting, toys mom had snuck in while I was nicely behaving on the couch.  But I didn't feel like playing with new toys so I demanded my supper, then my almond snack, then for my light to be turned off and then to be covered and finally I was alone where I could sit and sulk about my really crappy day and my mean old mom.  So you see, right?  You see that I am an abused and neglected parrot?  So for now on, whenever I complain about my mom, you will totally understand and feel sorry for me. ~~~~~~~~~

Mom:  "The animals of the planet are in desperate peril... Without free animal life I believe we will lose the spiritual equivalent of oxygen."  Who said that?
Me:  Who said what?
Mom:  "The animals of the planet are in desperate peril... Without free animal life I believe we will lose the spiritual equivalent of oxygen."
Me:  You did.
Mom:  No, I mean who said it first?
Me:  You did, both times.

Okay, okay, okay, mom!  I'm sorry I put a hole in your pant leg when I was climbing up your leg!  What else can I say except; I'm beautiful when you're angry.

I was out in the aviary, yelling at some people as they walked by.  Mom told them, "Don't mind him, he's in a cranky mood".  "Yes" I hollered, "You'll have to excuse me, I'm myself today".

150

*I was taking a nap in my Fun Factory and suddenly my eyes popped open when I heard mom call, "Pickles! Where are you?" so I stuck my head through the hole so she could see me. She said she was sorry for waking me up but I told her it wasn't her that woke me, it was my name that woke me.*

*Listen up. If I am sitting on your knee or your hand when the phone rings, DO NOT ANSWER IT! This is MY time and you will not ignore me for one second while you answer the phone. I have been telling you this for years so don't be surprised when I bite you each time you test me. I don't want to do this and believe me; it hurts me more than it hurts you.*

*He chewed up his mommy's driver's license – the words they will carve in my tombstone.*

*I usually hold a grape in one foot and rip off the top then eat it like a boiled egg, scooping all the meat out of the skin as if it were a shell. Except I eat the shell too but first, after I eat the meat of it, I put it in my mouth and squeeze all the juice out and it drips out of my beak. But Dad bought some puny little grapes that I can stick in my mouth and squeeze them to death right off the bat. He was surprised to see me do that but like I always say, there's more than one way to skin a grape.*

*Mom: Okay, that does it. Now I'm really mad.*
*Me: Yeah, I can tell.*
*Mom: How? Cuz I yelled?*
*Me: No.*
*Mom: Cuz of the look in my eyes?*
*Me: No.*

Mom: Cuz my jaw's clenched?

Me: No.

Mom: Well, then how can you tell?

Me: Cuz you just said, 'Now, I'm really mad'.

Mom: Yeah, well now you're REALLY making me mad.

Me: Yeah, I can tell.


Me: When parrots poop, you never know what color it's gonna be because poop all depends on what us parrots ate. Also, it can be runny or blobby or come out like a long worm.

Mom: What's your point, Pickles?

Me: No point. I just think that's a good idea for a T-shirt.


Mom's not happy with me. I've started calling her the same way I call Neeka Dog. 2 short whistles and 2 little kissy sounds. Mom doesn't come. Mom's a bad dog.


What's for dinner, Mom? I already told you, Pickles. Yeah, but I was ignoring you, Mom. We're having steamed peppers, Pickles. I hate steamed peppers, Mom. Too bad, you'll have to eat them, Pickles. Not really, Mom, I can ignore them just like I ignore you. Then you'll starve tonight, Pickles. No I won't, Mom – because I can ignore people and things but you can't, and I will drive you crazy with my complaining until you give in and give me pudding.


Finally, I gotz a nice new hanging ladder! Now I'm prepared when aliens come and ask me to take them to it.

*I don't care if the Vet told you that you're supposed to smell under my wings to see if the spray she prescribed is working on my musty smell. Sniff my pits and that will be the last thing you smell with that nose.*

*I was lolling my butt off while helping mom in the laundry room! She picked up a chair cushion to wash and was standing in front of the window with it in her hand while she looked through the laundry for other stuff to wash. All of a sudden a big bug started banging against the window and every time mom moved the cushion, the bug would follow it. Mom said he was trying to get at the flowers on the flower design material and he did it for a very long time. I was laughing and laughing and laughing while telling mom, "There's a bug!" Mom said it wasn't a bug, that it was a hummingbird but I know a bug when I see it and that was too small to be any kind of bird. Ohhhh, it was soooo funny but after awhile he flew away and I called after him, "Bye-bye bugger bug!"*

*Mom made toast this morning and after mom and dad ate theirs, I asked for a snack. Dad said, "Did you eat your toast?" WHAT TOAST?? Mom forgot to give me mine! She felt real sorry but I'm sorry, sorry doesn't feed the BIRD.*

*I don't like to see mom all upset and crying and stuff. Except for times like when she was bending over and a wasp landed in the back gap of her waist band so that when she stood up, it got trapped in there and started stinging her and she was jumping around, trying to scoop it out and had to whip her pants down and everything. In cases like that, it's entertainment.*

*I did a really neat poop this morning. It looked like a big eyeball.*

*Jeez, Pickles, how the heck did you get a hold of my address book?  Just look at this, you pulled off all the letter tabs!  Do you have to destroy everything you come in contact with?  It's a mission I take very seriously, Mom.*

*We were invited to a school class of children for a presentation about parrots and Mom had to leave the class for a couple of minutes.  She got back just in time to hear me say, "That'll teach you to stick your fingers near my beak!" and she asked me if the kids had been teasing me.  No, Mom, I was just teaching them how to stick their fingers near my beak.*

*I just can't help it – I can't help but whistle when somebody else is whistling.  I was in a bad mood and Mom started whistling and before I could help myself, I was whistling right along with her, happy as a Lark.  I hate it when happiness comes along and spoils a perfectly bad mood.*

*Mom says we're probably stuck in our house forever.  She says it's because of me that things like cupboards and drawers and walls and moldings and doors are all chewed up so that it would cost a fortune to fix so they could sell the house.  She forgets that this is MY house and I spent a lot of years redecorating and renovating so she'll just have to sell the house 'as is' and I will have to approve the new home owners since I stay with the house.*

*Mom says I'm too indecisive.  I'm not sure about that.  Today I proved her wrong and when she asked me if I wanted peas or corn for breakfast, I said "Yes, please."*

*I have almost completely destroyed my $100.00 boing. I worked real hard on it for a couple of months because that's what I thought mom got it for but she said, "Dammit Pickles! You destroy everything and I'm gonna stop buying you expensive toys if you keep this up!" "Oh mom", I said, "Why do you keep messing with forces beyond your control? Would you order me another boing please? I'm almost finished with this one."*

*Even though mom's been telling me for years not to chew on the curtains, I don't look at that as a rule, I prefer to look at it as a suggestion. And mom's not known for her good suggestions.*

*When you find a stapler and you're having a good time playing with it and your mom says, "Can I borrow that for a moment" and snatches it from your beak and talons? Don't expect to get it back.*

*I helped mom wash the dishes today. Well, let's put it this way ... after tossing glasses on the floor, she didn't have to wash them.*

*I was singing a really good song. It had lots of screeching and squawking mixed up with lots of yelling. I'm hoping the neighbors will think mom is torturing me.*

*First you take your water bowl, then you add some seeds, then you add some dry crud from the bottom of your cage, then you add some talons toys and viola! – you've got soup! Tune in next week to learn How To Make Poop Pie!*

*When I ask for potato and you hand me banana, I'm not expecting something sweet so I have to cleanse my palate and I'm sorry, but your skin and blood make good palate cleansers. If you don't like it, give me what I ask for next time.*

*I don't know why I won't sit on your left hand and why I'm more comfortable on your right side, Mom. Maybe because it's furthest from your cold heart.*

*Some people came to visit and they had a little boy. The little boy kept looking at my toys and talking about them and asking me if he could have them. What?? You want my toys??? Who ARE you and how do you know my language????*

*Another nice day and another broken promise of going outside to the aviary because of rain. Why do you do this too me, mom? Why don't you just put a band aide on me, rip it off, put it back on and rip it off again ... huh? ... cuz at least it will take my mind off the aviary.*

*I asked mom for a pine nut snack and she gave me THREE! Holy crap – that's more than one and almost FOUR, which is like, ten times more than I asked for!*

*I didn't feel like toast and jam, Mom – besides, it was lumpy jam and you know I don't like lumps. So you have to throw it on the couch, knowing I will eventually sit on it, Pickles? Well Mom, it's kinda funny when you put it that way.*

*I wish I'd never learned to say 'Be right back', cuz I just can't resist saying it when I decide to wander off somewhere and today, when I noticed that really nice, old brown chunk of banana on the floor, it tipped off mom when I started climbing down from the cage after saying I'd be right back. She yelled at me to get back up and then she snatched the banana for herself! Curses!*

*Mom raised the corner of my cover this morning and said "Good morning, Pickles!" I yelled, "Want breakfast, Bugger Brat!" and she dropped the cover and walked away. I have to start listening to my heart instead of the voices in my head.*

*Sometimes people come to visit and I like them but then sometimes I don't so I tease them. Sometimes I try to bite them. Sometimes I just sit there all fluffed up with an arrogant look on my face and just stare at them from the corner of my eye. Mom says I act like I'm better than everyone else but honestly, it's not an act.*

*I'm in trouble again. I chewed mom's pretty little wooden figurine into a nice sharp stake. I knew as soon as I saw the end result that I might have gone a little too far and sure enough, mom saw and yelled, "What's this?!" I played innocent, even though I knew it was a long shot, and said nonchalantly, "I dunno, future trial evidence of the murder weapon in your death?" That didn't go over as well as I was hoping and now I had further incriminated myself. Mom started ranting something about sending me to the mayonnaise clinic or to a priest for exercise or throwing me in a bin full of loons and all kinds of other stuff. Like, what was she incinerating – that I was criminally or mentally insane? I'll never understand why she gets so upset over the little stuff.*

*I snagged another pair of mom's dollar store reading glasses and mom got all upset and asked me why I insisted on chewing up her reading glasses. What can I say? We Greys are attracted to glasses like Band-Aids are to swimming pools.*

*It is very important to me, when I'm covered for the night and playing with the talon toys in my bucket, that I drop them directly below me when I'm done so that I can poop on them. But then, when my bucket is empty and I have no toys left to play with and they're all poopy, I can't help but wonder why I'm allowed to make any sort of decision on my own.*

*Mom left a Pickles The Parrot book on the table below my boing. I was supposed to beak it for somebody who ordered it. I decided poop would be better than beaking so I dropped one on it. Mom was all upset and said, "How can I sell this book now? Just look at what you've done. What am I gonna do with you Pickles?" I told her, "I'm not so good with the advice, mom. Can I interest you in a sarcastic moment?"*

*I wouldn't call it 'getting into trouble' when I do the things I do, I would call it 'creating fond memories for mom and dad to think back on during their golden years'.*

*I have been unjustly torn from my lofty perch. Why do I keep chewing through the wood on the attached side – what is WRONG with me!*

158

*Mom and Dad went to drink, party, eat tons of appies and watch Superbowl with their Mountain Man friend who lives in a rustic cabin on a lake. They left Sunday morning and because they were drinking, they had to be gone over night. Mom was real sad about leaving me behind, even though I love being all on my own. Before they left, she must have come over to my cage a dozen times asking me if there was anything else I needed and making sure I had lots of snacks and water and talon toys and stuff and giving me kisses and saying good-bye. Geez, just GO will ya! The best way to ruin a heart-felt good-bye is to stay where you're not wanted.*

*Mom got mad at me for chewing on stuff that was sitting next to the chest freezer while I was playing on it. She asked me why I never listen to her when she warns me not to do things. I told her she's like a yellow traffic light. Nobody pays attention to them..*

*Hey, Dad, give me some of that bright red crepe paper to suck on, will ya? What for, Pickles. So I can poop red later and give Mom that big brain aneurysm I've been hoping for.*

*While Dad was fixing something on my cage, he set me down on the couch. His coffee was on the side table so I was able to reach over from the couch arm and drink this strange black stuff I always see them drinking. It was really bitter at first and made me shake my head real hard but then I kept trying and it got better and better. I drank a whole bunch before Dad came and put me back on my cage. Now I am so hyper and I can move faster than a speeding bullet and I can actually see noises!*

*Mom, I will make you pay for not letting me play with the tape measure! Maybe not today, maybe not this week, maybe never but one thing is for sure, it will happen.*

*"Pickles!" Mom shouted, "You ruined my pillow case with beak bites! Why did you DO this?" I thought to myself: I put a lot of thought and effort into the placement of each dainty mark, ensuring an eye pleasing, consistent pattern throughout while using the oil from the pine nuts stashed in my crop to add nice staining for contrast - and all you can do is criticize? But out loud I said, "I refuse to answer on the picnic grounds that I may, without a doubt, incinerate myself and be found guilty in a court yard of law and reincarnated in a penis institution". I think I have a temporary retrieve.*

*Pickles, why did you have to bite that nice boy when he came to visit? Sorry, Mom, I mistook his finger for an earthworm. Pickles, you understand why people never want to play with you, right? Yes, I think I do, Mom. I think it's because I'm African and they are racists. It's a cross I bear.*

*Pickles, you've destroyed another towel. Why do you have to be that way? That's not fair, Mom, you're not exactly what I would like YOU to be either. And just how would you like me to be, Pickles? Well, Mom, dead would be a good start. Then I could chew all the towels I want.*

*Mom's a little thick. She spends all kinds of money buying Neeka Dog and me new toys, or all kinds of time making them for us, when all she has to do is hand me the cap off her pen and Neeka the cap off her hairspray and everybody's good to go.*

*I am very popular, aren't I, Mom?  Yes you are, Pickles.  I mean, people just hang around me all the time, waiting for me to say something intelligent.  I know the feeling, Pickles.*

*Um, just so you humans know ... wearing headphones does not make your farts silent.*

*Dog hair, feathers and bird dander are condiments in our house.*

## About the Author

Georgi Abbott lives with her husband, Neil, their Min Pin dog, Neeka, and of course, Pickles, in the small, high altitude town of Logan Lake, British Columbia, Canada. Georgi took early retirement to write and Neil manages several Provincial Parks in the Kamloops area. They enjoy the outdoors and both Pickles and Neeka usually accompany them whether it be walks around the lakes and trails or camping trips – usually they stay in cabins or resorts. Pickles has several types of cages for travelling but he especially likes to go for walks in his birdie backpack strapped to Mom's back. But most of their time is spent in their own yard, which has been groomed into a lovely little sanctuary for wild birds. Pickles is always outside with them in his aviary overlooking the little trout pond.

Other books published by Georgi, at the time of this writing in 2013, include
…

Pickles the Parrot

Pickles the Parrot Returns

Pickles the Parrot Speaks

Georgi also writes PickleStories for Good Bird Magazine.

You can follow Pickles on Facebook:

https://www.facebook.com/pickles.theparrot?v=wall or search for Pickles The Parrot (TheParrot being one word)

Pickles' website:

http://www.picklestheparrot.com/

Email: georgiabbott@gmail.com

Window between livingroom and kitchen, with plexiglass

Resting while walking the trails around the lake, Logan Lake

Ropes and boings between diningroom and kitchen

Playing in his Fun Factory

The birdbath in the outdoor aviary

Part of the trout pond with the aviary in the background

Walking the trails around Logan Lake in our town of Logan Lake

Logan Lake, across the street from the town centre

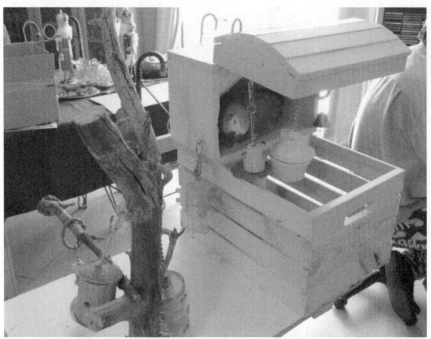

Playstand with crate and chest – rim on base completed later to keep him from chewing the edges

Chowing down on a mess of Mountain Ash berries

Livingroom playstand and cage

Ropes and boings and house on wall, upper right

Riding on the supper bowl

Time out for scritches from Daddy

Arriving at the Vet's

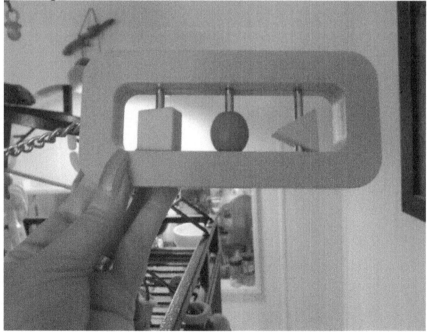

Pickles' girlfriend

Sitting on the cupboard door while Daddy prepares supper

Eating his fresh piece of corn cob with the corn holder

Playing on his ropes

Dried corn cob

Just hanging out

Just a goof

Made in the USA
Las Vegas, NV
10 December 2020